202 Outstanding
Modern Interior Designs

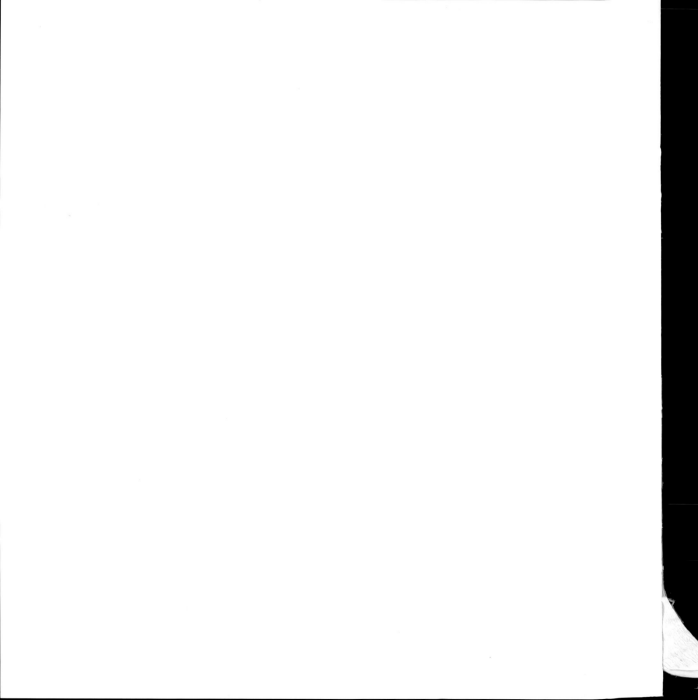

202 Outstanding
Modern Interior Designs

FIREFLY BOOKS

A FIREFLY BOOK

Published by Firefly Books Ltd. 2015

First printing

Publisher Cataloging-in-Publication Data (U.S.)

A CIP record for this title is available from the Library of Congress

Library and Archives Canada Cataloguing in Publication

A CIP record for this title is available from Library and Archives Canada

Published in the United States by
Firefly Books (U.S.) Inc.
P.O. Box 1338, Ellicott Station
Buffalo, New York 14205

Published in Canada by
Firefly Books Ltd.
50 Staples Avenue, Unit 1
Richmond Hill, Ontario L4B 0A7

Printed in Spain

6 LIVING ROOM

148 DINING ROOM

226 KITCHENS

372 BEDROOMS

462 BATHROOMS

544 OUTSIDE SPACES

LIVING ROOM

The living room is one of the most important spaces in a house. It is the meeting point for family and friends and where one can relax while reading, listening to music or watching television.

The living room is often the largest room in the house, so creating character with decorative details can prove difficult. One of the most common mistakes is forgetting that it is a room in which people spend a great deal of time and that the functionality of the furniture, the color, the materials and the lighting should meet the inhabitant's needs and tastes.

Originally, the living room was the place where guests were entertained — for a celebration or simply to chat and enjoy a cup of tea. This is still the case, but the use of this space has expanded — it is no longer purely a space for guests but has been adapted to meet the requirements of everyday life.

To create an attractive, functional living room, you need to know how the area will be used in order to decide what kind of furniture the space needs, what colors or combinations are most suitable and what sort of lighting is ideal. There should be plenty of seating in a living room. There are currently an infinite number of alternatives available: sofas, chairs, armchairs, stools and cushions are some of the many contemporary options for sitting around a coffee table, in front of the television or next to a large window, enjoying the view.

Shelving and storage units are useful to avoid unsightly clutter. A current trend is to combine old furniture with modern pieces. Another alternative is to install versatile elements that can be placed anywhere in the room, guaranteeing a completely unique setting. Combining pragmatic aspects with personal taste helps to create atmosphere in a living room. The decor should be daring but practical.

Choosing strong colors can create a sophisticated air, whereas light or neutral tones will produce a more serene ambiance. Remember that dark colors will reduce the light, so additional lighting should be incorporated into reading areas or darker spaces.

Lighting is always important in the living room. The placement of lighting elements will depend on the levels of illumination in the room, whether natural or artificial. Windows or skylights are important to allow natural light into the house.

If the layout allows, the dining room can be incorporated into the living room, and both can be integrated with the kitchen. Combining the functions of these spaces provides a quick solution for an informal family lunch or breakfast, helping day-to-day organization and avoiding the need to move food from one room to another. With this kind of alternative arrangement, the materials, shapes and colors are important.

The proposals featured here include living rooms that are connected to the dining room, others that are a continuation of a home office and some that integrate the dining room and the kitchen by using similar decorative elements. There are thousands of arrangement alternatives, but you need to consider the technical limitations of your property before deciding the best way to use your space.

9

11

© Diego Opazo

001 Old recesses are both practical and decorative, and modern interior design can find or create many uses for them. You can install a light within them, according to what you want to use them for and the effect you want to create with the items located inside.

002

With the advent of modern heating systems the use of fireplaces is in decline, especially in urban homes. But rather than doing away with them, you can transform them into an important decorative element in the living room.

© Morten Odding

© Donna Griffith

003

Rather than conjuring up images of antiquated, rustic or industrial buildings, by combining reclaimed brick walls in a living room with carefully chosen furnishings, textiles and materials, you can create a warm and welcoming atmosphere. Strategically located in any room, it will become the focal wall and give character and personality to the space.

© Martin Tessler

© Martin Tessler

© Martin Tessler

004 Glass provides views of the surrounding landscape and should be used whenever the architecture permits. Here, the large, slanted windows provide views of the sky and let in light that provides clarity to the entire space.

23

© Geoffrey Hodgdon

005

Carpets are an effective decorative element.
They dress any room elegantly, give a sense
of warmth, provide good insulation and can
be a good way of marking different spaces.

© Geoffrey Hodgdon

© Hervé Abbadie

006   There should always be plenty of seating in a living room. In this house, a comfortable sofa is complemented with yellow "butterfly" chairs, which combine with the ocher tone of the wall tapestry.

© Hervé Abbadie

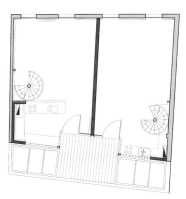

007 Placing a half-height wall is an effective way of separating the kitchen and living-dining room, without losing the light that comes in from the terrace. The spiral staircase becomes a decorative object within this space.

© Hervé Abbadie

008 Lighting and views of outside always influence the mood of the room. Whether alone or with friends and family, it is important to feel content and relaxed in the living room. Gentle colors, such as those chosen here, are an excellent option.

© Hervé Abbadie

Here, the colors chosen and the simple lines of the furniture create a living room that is perfectly balanced. None of the elements take precedence over the others.

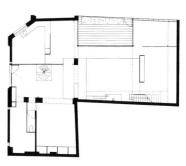

009

Choosing furniture with simple lines and shapes, and using mostly white and light tones creates a clean and uncluttered space that conveys a feeling of tranquillity.

The interior design of this house integrates the furniture with the architecture, which maintains aspects of the original structure, such as the roof beams.

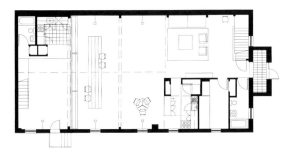

A mustard color has been chosen in order to contrast with the white walls. The second story of the house appears above the living room, protected by a wooden railing that marks the horizontal line.

35

All the details of this space emphasize its linearity. The living and dining rooms are characterized by a light effect in which cool materials dominate, and glass surfaces contrast with black and white tones.

010 Large areas enable a clear distribution of spaces. The bedroom in this house has an unusual location, behind a concrete wall that separates it from the living room.

011 Maintaining some elements of the original architecture gives a living room character. In this case, the wooden doors with their original handles, have been kept, along with the interior concrete columns.

This large living room is bathed in light, which enters through the big windows. A system of drapes separates the communal area from the private area when necessary.

© Joy Von Tiedemann

An old cart has been used as a coffee table in this living room. The dining room table and chairs are also older pieces that belong to the owner and have been restored.

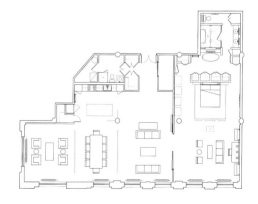

012 Living room windows need to provide plenty of light, although we also need systems for reducing the amount of natural light when necessary. Lightweight linen curtains can be used to filter the light during the hours when it is most intense.

© Jordi Miralles

013 It is important to consider the layout of the property when deciding where to place the living room. In this attic, the living room is located under the slope of the roof to make the most of the available space and of the light coming in through the skylights.

This house has been structured according to the characteristics of the building. The kitchen, for example, has been located at one end, in front of windows that let in natural light.

45

© Eduardo Girão

© Eduardo Girão

© Célia Weiss

014 When defining the lighting in a room you need to be very clear about the kind of atmosphere you want to create. If you want to convey warmth, lighting should be subdued and indirect, with the various light sources strategically located.

© Célia Weiss

015

Although using animal print in interior design may be a risky proposition, using these motifs in the correct quantities guarantees a luxurious result. Animal prints combine well with neutral colors such as off-white, beige, sand and black. Use fabric or leather with animal print on armchairs, decorative cushions, rugs, bedclothes, carpets and so on.

© Antonie Bootz, Costa Picadas

© Alain Brugier

016

When choosing furniture for your living room, always think about creating a special place in which to relax, read or watch television. Here a wood and leather recliner fulfils that need, strategically placed in front of the patio so as to relax and enjoy the views.

© Henrique Barros-Gomes/HBG

017 To help intergrate different areas but also create a certain independence between them, alternate warm spaces in which simple shapes predominate with sparsely decorated rooms. This produces a simple composition.

The fireplace occupies the central space in this living room but does not affect the continuity of the artwork above it.

© John Gollings

The initial concept for this small, urban apartment aimed to create a connection between the rooms with decorative details such as color.

© Matthijs van Roon

018 In a minimalist space, with a predominance of straight-lined furniture with lots of white and cool shades, inserting a fireplace as a central element can bring warmth and an interesting color contrast.

© Mark Arbeit

The table in the work area extends to a wall that houses a fireplace. The spaces exude warmth with their simple composition and perfectly combined materials.

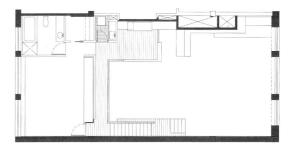

© Maoder Chou

019

This L-shaped kitchen houses the stove, sink, countertops and cabinets, ending in a table that creates a workspace. This is a good idea when trying to keep a kitchen open to different uses.

© Virginia del Giudice

© Virginia del Giudice

020 When spaces are free from superfluous decorative elements, it is easy to circulate between rooms. Dark walls, furniture and carpets absorb a lot of light.

The double-story height of this home enables the communal spaces to be placed on the lower floor and the bedrooms and other private areas on the upper level.

021

By using a set of comfortable chairs instead of large sofas in a living room, you can create more versatility in the room, allowing for it to be easily rearranged as well as creating a greater sensation of space.

© Véronique Mati

022

Making the most of outdoor space and integrating it within the interior space as though it were a painting or a photograph is another decorative tool that can be used when the environment allows. Here, the green of the ivy on one side creates the perfect contrast with the brick wall and the warm colors of the living room, while coordinating with the small decorative objects on the table.

© Jacob Sadrak

Here, the contemporary furnishings and gentle lighting create a functional, uniform space that is easy to negotiate.

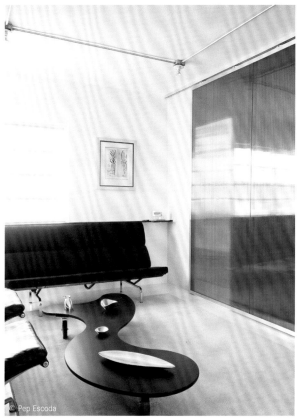

023 To keep a space from looking boring, add a touch of lightness and freshness by introducing a note of color that breaks up the predominant chromatic scheme. Here, a blue sliding door separates the bathroom from the living room.

© Virginia del Giudice

024   A pass-through facilitates the connection
between the kitchen and the living area,
while promoting interaction between people
in these rooms. A roll-up shutter offers the
possibility to connect adjacent spaces or
separate them according to the needs.

© Fabien Baron

025 Hardwood floors and strong colors are a good way to create a space with contrasts that is also warm. The combination of light and dark lends the room a sophisticated air.

© Fabien Baron

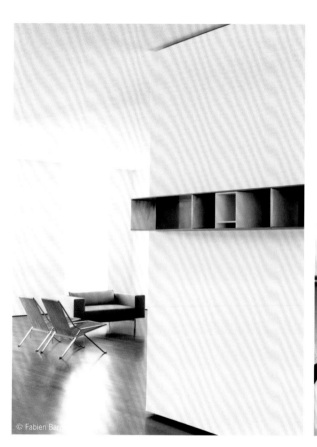

© Fabien Baron

© Fabien Baron

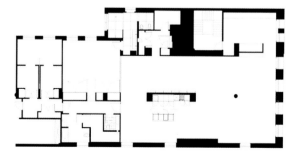

This space stands out because of its classical arrangement. Simple, elegant, cool lines are combined with contemporary seating alternatives and coffee tables that are not suitable for dining.

© Alberto Peris Caminero

026 In this house, all the spaces coexist perfectly.
The use of light tones and cool materials,
such as the transparent surfaces, enhance the
spatial fluidity and link the rooms seamlessly.

The objective of this living room was to create a lookout point for the surrounding views. The placement of the two "butterfly" chairs enables maximum enjoyment of the panorama.

© Sharrin Rees

© Sharrin Rees

© Tuca Reinés

© Tuca Reinés

027 Rather than hiding spaces behind curtains, fill areas with glass surfaces, to create an open interior that offers views of the exterior.

This chromatic scheme has been limited to black and white, with smooth surfaces that enhance the professional design of the space. Emphasizing the industrial aspect creates an elegant and sophisticated look.

© Tuca Reinés

© Tuça Reinés

028 This living room is separated from the
dining room and kitchen by a glass partition
that insulates it from any noise. It is also
a good option to prevent kitchen odors
from spreading throughout the home and
to create a space that is connected to the
yard outside.

The interior and exterior are diluted: nature is invited in. Furthermore, the house's modular design means the construction does not harm the environment.

© Torfi Agnarsson

© Luis Ros

According to the architects, this house was
designed as a "landscape of lineal events" that
fold out onto the lot and form an ascending spiral.
The closed longitudinal façades act as beams and
create a projection of about 50 feet (15 m).

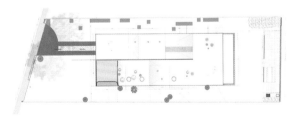

© Luis Ros

© Hiroyuki Hirai

A ledge marks the length of the deck, which is located above the countryside like a lookout post. A staircase leads to the upper level, which houses the bedrooms and bathroom.

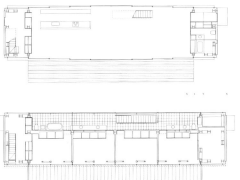

© Hiroyuki Hirai

© Hiroyuki Hirai

© Hiroyuki Hirai

029 The evocative image of the surrounding forest extends into the interior of this house, which blends into the landscape. If trying to create a feeling of freedom, installing large windows will produce a sense of space.

030

Choosing a good sofa takes time and thought. Not only do you need to consider color and shape, but the balance between design and comfort must also be absolute. Here, the blue adds a touch of color, which breaks the predominant color base, the velvet adds warmth to the space and the L-shaped design also helps to separate the living and dining areas.

© Vincent van den Hoven

© Laziz Hamani

031 Architecture helps when it comes to finding the best furniture arrangement. This room is dominated by its huge windows and the spectacular views they offer. The dining room is also arranged so as to make the most of the impressive natural light.

© Peter Joshua Lawrence

© Peter Joshua Lawrence

032

Wonderful contrasts can be achieved through the use of different materials, with very different textures maintaining a colorful harmony without being garish.

© Cynthia van Elk

033 The furniture is made from recycled materials such as wine boxes or furniture, and the same goes for the lights. Minimal budget but maximum design aesthetic.

034

The careful placement of a single item can fill a room on its own and add character. Leaving behind convention, you can create eclectic spaces in which the mix of objects enriches the room and gives it its own distinct personality.

© Marco Antônio

© João Morgado – Architecture Photography

The house has no transition zones: the living room is the nucleus and separates the master suite from the rest of areas. There is space. It is insistently minimalist.

© Carola Ripamonti

© Jean Bourbon

035   Before decorating your living room consider
how you will be using it. Think about what
kind of furniture, decorative elements and
accessories you are going to need in order
to create a room to your taste, in your own
personal style.

When spaces are renovated, the layout can be changed and the living room can be placed in the optimum location. Maintaining original construction details and combining them with contemporary pieces creates a neo-rural design.

© Luis Hevia

© Alan Gastelum

© Héctor Santos-Díez, BISimages

036 Sometimes creating a feeling of spaciousness in a rectangular area is not an easy task. Choosing simple, lightweight and low-rise furniture that gives way to large, bare walls is an effective solution. Remember not to overload the room with too much furniture.

© Laurent Saint Jean | 3MILLE

037 If you are fortunate enough to have a living
room with large picture windows, you should
aim to arrange your furniture so as to gain
maximum benefit from the landscape and
allow for plenty of light to flood in – especially
important for reading and work areas.

© Ondrej Synak

© Ondrej Synak

© Ionna Roufopoulou

© Estudio Teresa Sapey

038 Industrial buildings guarantee open spaces
with different furniture positioning options.
Here the glass separators enhance the
communication between the different areas.

© Carola Ripamonti

© Fran Parente

039 Your choice of furniture depends on the size of your space. Here, the high ceilings have provided enough room for a network of shelves that extends the full length of the living-room wall. The top shelves are best reached by ladder.

040

To create vivid spaces you need to skilfully combine unpretentious old furniture with more modern pieces. Here the retro sofas in Scottish fabric and leather are coordinated with a wide, white-lacquered bookcase with pure, clean lines, which houses a large plasma TV.

© Barbara Bonomi, Gabriele Gatta

© CJ Isaac

041 The materials emphasise the warmth that the owners are seeking in each room. Thus a balanced coexistence is established between woods, fabrics and colors. In this very straight-lined, contemporarily furnished room, the brown shades and materials selected create an atmosphere of serene warmth.

042 Staircases have been making their
mark on decorating plans, going from
being simple elements for walking up or
downstairs to being the focal point of a
room. Instead of going unnoticed, they have
been transformed into the backbone that
connects the two floors of the house and
their design must be consistent with the
atmosphere you want to create.

043

You can create space, light, depth and continuity within a room according to how you use a mirror. Mirrors work well in small rooms as they visually expand the space, whereas in a dark room a mirror helps to reflect the light and make it brighter.

© Tom Ross of Brilliant Creek

© Daniel Levin

044 Lighting can be a good way of separating areas in large spaces. Here, the positioning of the lighting points in the ceiling clearly defines the living and dining areas.

123

© Zecc Architecten

© Zecc Architecten

045 Mixing old and new is usually a safe bet. Here, the combination of new, straight-lined pieces with vintage items looks even better thanks to the space and brightness of the room.

© Valentino Bellini

046   When white becomes a second skin and dresses a space entirely, it guarantees a bright interior. The effect is enhanced still more if the room benefits from a lot of natural light.

© Gianni Franchellucci

047 An attractive and impactful piece of artwork can be the key decorative element of a room. Here, the strength of the painting that presides over the living room sets off the color palette used: on a neutral base the predominance of red as a point of contrast is evident.

© Gianni Franchellucci

131

© Luigi Filetici

© Tim Griffith

048

In an open space, different levels on the floor and ceiling can work well for separating different areas. Here, the difference in level both in the floor and in the ceiling defines the transition from living room to dining room with absolute clarity.

© i29 I interior architects

049   Books always create a welcoming
atmosphere. If you cannot have a bookcase,
use a shelf or little corner to bring this touch
of warmth to the room.

© Philippe Harden

050 When renovating an old house it is a good idea to preserve the original wood flooring. A renovated wooden floor has a beautiful shine to it that cannot be matched by a newly made hardwood floor. It is also better quality for two reasons: in times gone by there was an abundance of wood in relation to the population so only the best woods were used to make boards. Secondly, as the timber ages, its humidity reduces and it becomes more stable.

© Roman Shishak

© Eugeni Bach

051 A base of light colours works well in small rooms, as does the use of materials of the same type, creating more continuity and harmony within the space. If you want to break up the uniformity of color and materials you can use lamps or other decorative elements that serve as a point of contrast.

052 Using ceramic or clay tiles on the floor works very well in warm climates due to their physical characteristics. As they are cold materials with high thermal inertia, they can be cooling in the summer while accumulating large amounts of heat in the winter. They are also very strong and durable, and easy to maintain.

© Davide Arena

053

Ordering a custom bookcase is always advantageous. It adapts perfectly to the room's existing architectural elements such as the windows and radiators. It can also be designed specifically to suit the items that it is going to house, such as books, CDs, television and music system, meaning that everything is better organized. To create more of a feeling of spaciousness in small areas it is a good idea to paint the bookcase in the same color as the walls.

© Stefano Pedretti

054

By combining LED strip lamps with conventional lamps and spotlights we can create a special, intimate atmosphere that is full of personality yet also saves all-important energy. LED lights do not emit heat, which avoids wasting energy and enables them to be used in small and delicate spaces where such heat could be harmful.

© Stefano Pedretti

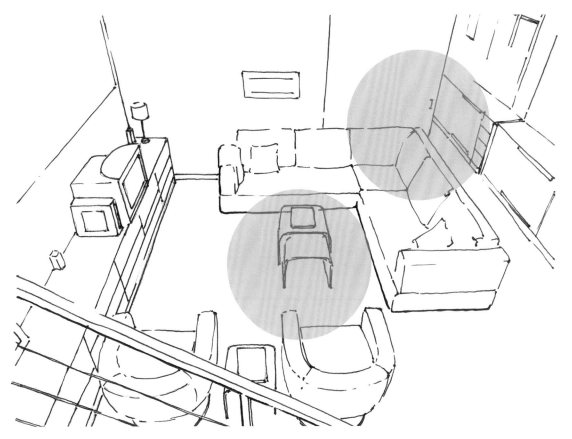

055 The expressive possibilities of artificial lights are infinite, and the location of spotlights can help define different areas. Coffee and accent tables are useful for occasional meals. You can create a private space in a living room with a sliding door, which is the most flexible solution for dividing a room.

056

Natural light is always better than artificial light, as it is cheaper, healthier and more environmentally friendly. The arrangement of the lighting and furniture will depend on how the room will be used. In this case, the fireplace dictates the placement of the sofas. Double-story open-concept designs have the advantage that space can also be distributed vertically.

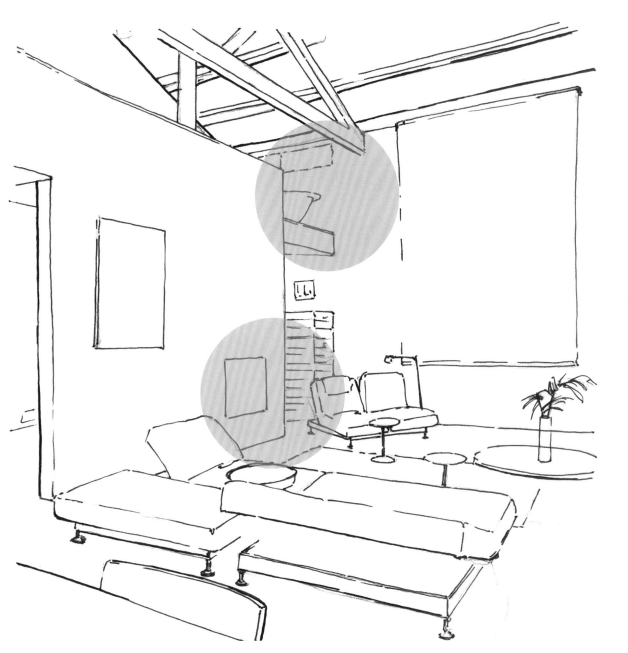

057 Contemporary seating alternatives are multiple: chaise lounges, armchairs, sofas, stools, large cushions. There should never be a lack of seating in a living room. Maintaining details of the original structure, such as exposed pipes, reinforces the industrial character of the space.

DINING ROOM

Not so long ago, dining rooms were considered the most formal part of the home. Perhaps the domestic space with the most rigid function, dining rooms were only used on special occasions, be it a holiday meal or a dinner party. The rest of the time they were left idle, with a polished dining table waiting anxiously in anticipation.

Trends in the way we eat have led us to rethink the dining room. A rising food culture and appreciation of a healthy diet mean dining rooms are no longer reserved for dinner parties. Dining rooms have been incorporated into the main part of the home and afforded, when possible, light and space, the principal elements of well-being.

That said, the dining room is perhaps the least flexible room in terms of decoration. Tables and chairs are its principal features, together with a cabinet or some other form of storage that provides easy access to the implements needed for eating. Lofts and studios rarely have a separate room available for dining, and, therefore, many owners forgo a table altogether. This is a common mistake. Although eating at a counter or on your lap can be fun occasionally, a table, however small or simple, is a fundamental necessity for entertaining. Nothing beats sitting around a table and bonding over food, a bottle of wine and good conversation. Those who live in small spaces should look at other ways to save on space (such as elevated beds) in order to be able to fit a table into their apartment.

Those with a little more space — but not enough for the luxury of a designated dining room — often incorporate a table into the kitchen. Although this is a highly practical solution, remember that this table will be used for all types of dining occasions. Therefore, give a little forethought to lighting, table accessories and other elements that will make the area adaptable. A kitchen table can be converted into an intimate dining setting with a stylish tablecloth and a few candles, and by dimming the lighting in the preparation areas.

The principles of adaptability should also apply in the main dining room. Any room that is seldom used is a waste of space, so make sure your table and chairs serve other purposes. A dining table can double as a work space for sewing, writing or any other activity. Centerpieces should be easy to move and clean. Floor coverings should also be low maintenance. Carpets and rugs are simply not practical when there is food around, unless they are specifically made for the kitchen or dining room. If your dining room has no direct access to your kitchen area, install a cupboard for your plates, cutlery and glasses. Movable carts are also handy if you like to entertain; rarely is a dining table large enough to accommodate a table setting and serving bowls with ease. Lighting should come from above, to enhance the food and the sheen of the plates and glasses, and reduce eyestrain between the diners. An extra floor lamp or a lamp placed on your sideboard can provide additional lighting.

Your choice of table and chairs will be dictated by your needs, the space available and your personal taste. Although the trend is for oversized tables, this is not a good choice for single people and couples unless they entertain frequently. Retractable tables — either those that provide some extra space when needed or that can be folded vertically when not in use — are enjoying a renaissance. Go for a stylish, well-made model that is easily retracted. Many tables also come with a built-in storage element (normally in the form of a lift-off top), and thses are an excellent solution in small spaces.

Dining chairs should be both stylish and comfortable — nothing can ruin a dining experience quite as much as an uncomfortable chair. Sets are best, as even the most carefully chosen one-offs are rarely the same height. If you think you may need to bring in extra seating from the kitchen or other areas for dinner parties, make sure they complement your dining chairs in terms of both design and height. Folding chairs are also a practical solution.

Personalizing your dinner table is one of the joys of entertaining. Place mats, napkins, cutlery and dinnerware come in an infinite range of styles and colors. Don't overdo your table: set out what is needed and bring in other elements when they're needed. Flowers are still the most popular table adornment, but instead of placing a large vase in the center, experiment with small individual flower arrangements or even a single flower incorporated into the design of each individual setting.

058

Choose your dining table to match your needs. People who live alone or with their partner need, at most, a four-seat model. Families, however, will need to choose a larger model, preferably rectangular, that can also double as a workspace.

Tom Ross of Brilliant Creek

059

An outdoor, semi-enclosed dining area is ideal, as it allows you to take advantage of most weather conditions. However, if it is the only dining area, it is only practical if the kitchen is within easy, convenient reach.

© Barclay & Crousse

© Yoshiharu Matsumura

This dining room is in a glass-enclosed attic, offering fabulous urban views. Polished wood and white furniture lend the composition a distinct Scandinavian feel.

© Yoshiharu Matsumura

060 Don't clutter your dining table with too many chairs. Place the minimum number of chairs for your everyday needs around the table and keep spare ones stored away. Don't place a table against a wall (unless it is particularly easy to move), as this will give some diners a "dead" view.

A white modular dining set works harmoniously with this spectacular convex glass wall overlooking the backyard. The concave interior wall encloses the composition.

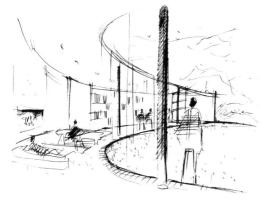

061 If possible, place your dining table close to a natural light source. Extra lighting, preferably a chandelier pendant light or other overhead fixture that can be adjusted to different heights, should be well placed. Avoid lighting that will obstruct the view.

© Katsuhisa Kida/fototeca

160

© Katsuhisa Kida/fototeca

This space has a somewhat industrial feel and is
distributed over three stories that are accessed by
a staircase that defines the vertical composition.

062 This house was designed for maximum integration with its surroundings. To achieve this, the walls are glass, affording views of the yard and creating a connection between the exterior and interior.

© Ross Honeysett

This furniture arrangement follows the rectangular shape of this open-plan loft. The dining area is located directly next to the kitchen, and there is a large coffee table in the living area.

© Stefano Graziani

© Karina Iliovska

063

Your choice of table is one of the key elements in dining-room design. Ideally it will be centrally positioned with enough room for free movement within the space. The size of the space available should dictate the shape and size of your table. Your style can come from the wall colors, the accompanying furniture or from your chosen table itself.

064

If your room is small, put a mirror on one of the walls to extend the depth of vision. If there is no natural light this will also brighten up the space. For best effect, hang it at the height of the chairs.

© hoo

© Cynthia van Elk

065 Chandeliers are a key element in dining rooms and often become the focal point, adding character to the room. But remember, when you are choosing, to think about its function and size, as well as its design aesthetic.

Defining the dining area with a transparent panel fits in this retro-inspired decor perfectly. The transparency of the dining chairs and striking light feature, together with the neutral color tones, give the room a sophisticated air and save it from falling into the realm of kitsch.

© Darius Ramazani

© Marc Mormeneo

066 Even the smallest lofts or studios need a
table. A common mistake is thinking that a
coffee table will suffice. This is not the case.
Look at ways to make space available, such
as this retractable bed (see at right), and find
dining chairs comfortable enough to be your
main seating.

This compact studio cleverly combines kitchen, dining and sleeping areas. The bed can be folded away when not in use, behind screens that are as attractive as they are useful.

© Satoshi Asakawa/zoom

Although strikingly minimalist, this eating area has all the traditional components of a classic dining room: a table, chairs and a cabinet in which to store dishes and cutlery.

© Satoshi Asakawa/zoom

177

© Ross Honeysett

067 Dining and living areas can also be defined with furniture. Here, a long rectilinear sofa acts as a dividing wall and matches the dimensions of the dining room table. Keep surfaces and walls stark for a truly minimalist visual theme.

© Ionna Roufopoulou

068 A bench works well for optimizing space. Although it may not be the most comfortable, it means there is space to seat three people when before there was room for only two chairs. As well as being practical it also has a decorative function, as it breaks the aesthetic of the traditional dining room.

© Luis da Cruz

069 If you have the space, a dining area in the
kitchen can be a wonderful attribute in a
house, allowing diners and cooks to be
together while food is being prepared. This is
also useful for families, as children need to be
monitored constantly while they are eating.

070 Meals with family and friends often result in long and deep after-dinner discussions. Positioning the table in front of the fireplace can be a good alternative to its usual place in the living room, and creates a warm and familiar atmosphere.

© Peter Landers

© Tyson Reist

071

Glass-top tables are ideal for formal meals, but they should be avoided in family homes. They are also useful for small spaces as their transparency and reflective qualities make the room feel larger.

072 A half-height wall works well in industrial spaces that are wide and open. It can hide the kitchen from the main dining room without losing the characteristic sense of space.

185

© Juan David Fuertes Fotografía

© Juan David Fuertes Fotografía

Stripping back a wall to stone, installing a wooden
floor and choosing a white lacquer for another wall
was all it took to make the interior friendly.

© Francesco Di Gregorio

073 Food can only be enhanced with natural light
and views, even if it means locating the table
further from the kitchen. Create a different
ambience at night with well-designed lighting.

074 A lack of space in today's homes means we often need rooms to perform more than one function and get the most out of every piece of furniture. Thus in a dining room the table may have a dual purpose –as a study table and as a dining table– and a bookcase, depending on its design, might also be part-pantry, for storing utensils and table linen.

© Michael Moran

075 Large natural-wood tables with a rustic feel are ideal, either combined with traditional chairs or in a more modern style. Moreover, these pieces are often made from reclaimed wood planks, which has the added benefit of being environmentally friendly.

076

If there is room, a cabinet to store dishes, table decorations and other important items can save the effort of retrieving them from the kitchen, as well as adding more interest to your dining room with an extra piece of furniture.

© i29 I Interior Architects

077

If your kitchen and dining room are closely connected, use complementary color and texture in your main furnishings to achieve harmony in your decor. In this loft, the table and chairs combine perfectly with the black lacquer and wood profile finish of the cupboards.

© Takumi Ota

© CJ Isaac

078   Define your dining space with a rug. This is the easiest way to differentiate it within a single living area, and also serves to add warmth.

© Alain Brugier

079

What used to be a risky proposition no longer is: mixing is all the rage and today just about anything goes, as long as the result demonstrates harmony in its colors and shapes. Leather chairs combine with metal, plastic models are mixed with wood...variety is the spice of life.

© Frank Hanswijk

© Stefano Pedretti

080 To decorate a dining room in contemporary style, when it comes to colors plain ones are best, such as white, black and gray. These three shades can be combined with little details in other, more vivid colors such as maroons, reds, oranges and purples.

© Stefano Pedretti

© Antonie Bootz, Costa Picadas

© Eduardo Girão

081 To avoid giving up your mini office, one good idea is to install a bar where you can eat breakfast, lunch and dinner in the tranquillity of your kitchen. It is also very versatile. For example, if your kitchen is open to the living room it can be a good way of separating the different areas and giving them their independence.

082

A soft color palette is the best option for decorating a small room, for example ivory, pale yellow and white. This does not mean, however, that you cannot use strong or dark colors —these can be used on small details to give them prominence.

© Jiři Ernest

083

Round tables and small dining rooms are great allies. Tables of this shape can fit in any corner, they are practical and they can make the room feel larger. They can also accommodate extra guests.

© Livio Marrese

084

The careful blend of bright colors, the decorating of walls with artworks and the unusual design of the lights creates a poetic space that tells a thousand stories.

© Spazio 14 10: Giulia Peruzzi

© Spazio 14 10: Giulia Peruzzi

© Vassilis Makris

085   Every corner of the house needs a different form of lighting. To give a dining room a warm and intimate feel, try using one or more ceiling-mounted hanging lamps for a focused and enveloping light source. This is especially useful in rooms that have more than one function, to separate the dining room from the rest of the space.

© Victor Núñez / Mauricio Fuertes

© Mark Arbeit

A picture hangs in the dining room, adding an
artistic touch.

© Steve Schappacher & Rhea White

086 Coffee tables can work as dining tables if the seating arrangement is adjusted accordingly. A wide range of low seating, such as cushions and stools, is now available, meeting the current demand for a less formal way of dining.

087 The dining table can be placed against the kitchen furnishings or in its own area. A powerful range hood will prevent cooking smells from spreading. Two-story spaces are ideal for separating communal and private areas. Dividing panels are a good way to separate different areas.

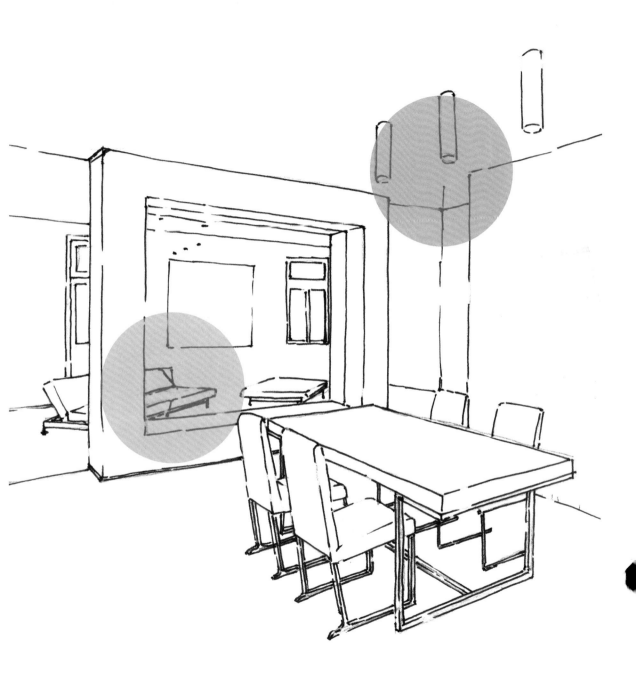

088 To prevent heat and smoke from reaching the dining room, this kitchen is closed in an L-shape and has an extractor fan that eliminates odors. The perimeter of the staircase has been used as storage and houses drawers. When the kitchen is in the middle of the central space, the use of different warm and cool colors can contribute to the separation of the areas.

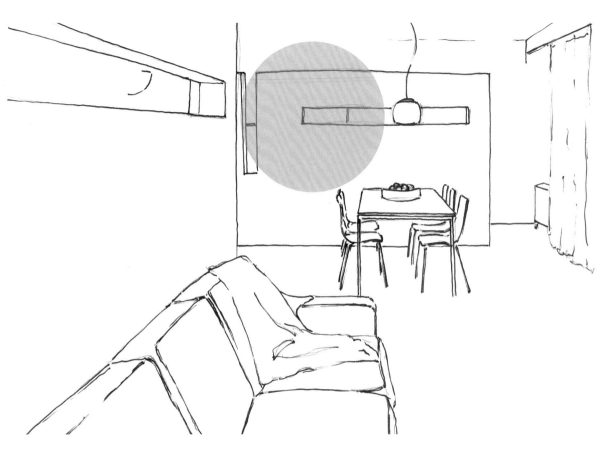

089 Separations between areas are functional when they are practical, simple and straightforward. There are now excellent alternatives to the classic folding screen. The view from the dining room should be uncluttered. The small openings in this separation panel let people communicate between the different rooms.

KITCHENS

In ancient times, the kitchen hearth was the heart of the home. With the rise of the upper class in the 19th century, this changed. The kitchen was downsized and consigned to a basement or an isolated, dark corner, becoming the domain solely of servants. Nowadays, the food and nutrition culture is ever more popular, and the kitchen area is now more important than ever. It has gone beyond a mere place to prepare food and become somewhere to meet, converse and bond.

Contemporary kitchen designs can be achieved in even the most space-challenged urban apartments, as new technology intelligently fuses form and function. Ovens are now neat and compact, glass ceramic stovetops fit flush into counters and refrigerators can be ordered with doors to match the rest of your cabinets. Entirely self-contained units can be tucked away behind double doors and closed off from the rest of the living area in an instant.

Of course, space is a luxury, and if you have it, dedicate a good part of it to a generous open-plan kitchen. Centrally placed carts and islands can accommodate extra storage, a counter, a dining area, a sink or even a cooking appliance.

Kitchens are generally arranged around the classic "U" or "L" shape. The varied use of most kitchens means you need to take many factors into account at the initial planning stage. Analyze how you work and plan accordingly. As a general rule, the kitchen needs to be divided into preparation, storage and dining areas, with enough space between to move unhindered. Do you need a kitchen table or can you easily take prepared food to a separate dining area? Perhaps a breakfast bar or freestanding counter is sufficient for your needs? Families need plenty of storage; think about which cabinets you want your children to have access to and which you don't, and then organize the space accordingly. If possible, dedicate an area within the kitchen as a play area or space where kids can do their homework (away from the cooking area). A discreet flat-screen television in the kitchen is another option to keep kids entertained while you work.

Given the number of gadgets and appliances we use in a kitchen these days, planning sufficient electrical outlets is vital. This cannot be stressed enough, as potentially dangerous extension cords should be avoided in the kitchen at all costs. When space is tight, some choose to put the washing machine in the kitchen area, in which case plumbing needs to accommodate this as well as a sink and dishwasher.

Natural light and ventilation are particularly important in the kitchen. An external window will make fumes and cooking smells disappear more quickly — and in a more eco-friendly way — than a range hood (although both are often necessary), and natural light is ideal for food preparation, so don't block it with furniture or other objects. That said, site-specific spotlighting is generally needed. Make sure there is sufficient light for working at your kitchen appliances by installing spots on the underside of overhead cabinets. Most good range hoods have lights incorporated, which are vital for correct and efficient cooking.

In terms of materials, the modern kitchen designer is spoiled for choice. Counters and cabinets come in an infinite variety of colors and finishes. Sinks are available in ceramic and stainless steel, and even large appliances, such as refrigerators and dishwashers have become design elements. Faucets are now elegant and decorative. Floor coverings should be resilient, non-slip and easy to clean. Stone and ceramic tile floors are ideal. If you opt for wood, make sure it is a hard-wearing variety and protect the area around the sink with a water-resistant covering. Don't discount good old-fashioned linoleum; modern designs and color schemes make it a stylish, low-cost alternative.

But even the most modern kitchens require a personal touch. Contemporary food culture has produced a myriad of items and accessories that can help you personalize your kitchen. Textiles, plants and flowers, spice jars, storage baskets and bowls can all add color and character. Even appliances can make a statement, as can a row of cookbooks or a selection of gourmet food products. The trick to a truly successful kitchen is to personalize it after making sure it is completely functional. So plan well first, then have fun decorating the heart of your home.

© Roman Shishak

© Jiří Ernest

© Carola Ripamonti

090

When choosing chairs for the kitchen it is a good idea to opt for material that is easy to clean, such as polypropylene or metal, as steam and grease can stick to porous materials such as wood and some upholstery. Polypropylene chairs such as those in this photo are noted for their strength, making them ideal for everyday use and their modern design, with delicate curves, also makes cleaning them easy.

© Gianni Franchellucci

© Hervé Abbadie

This awkward, hemmed-in space (on a ground floor and below a stair case) has been cleverly converted into a kitchen. The apple-green wall element defines the room, yet it also creates a connection with the upper floor and adjacent living area.

© Catherine Tighe

091

Doing away with doors and incorporating walls with cutouts can integrate the kitchen into the rest of the home yet still define its separate function.

© Eduard Hueber

092 Consider a custom-made piece, such as
this spectacular freestanding cabinet, if your
budget and space allow. Here it provides an
extra preparation and storage area.

© Eduard Hueber

093 Using different types of wood and wood finishes can create a warm yet dramatic interplay. A hard-wearing wood should be used for high-traffic kitchen floors, in a dark color or stain to hide dirt.

© RES4

094 The most notable change in kitchen design
over recent decades has been the union of
kitchen with living and dining room. If you
can, take down the walls or join the
rooms with dual-purpose elements
and service areas.

© Joshua Mchugh

This spectacular alcove-type structure holds all the functional components of the kitchen in one unit. Extra storage space is provided in the freestanding cabinet opposite, whereas the dining table provides a more formal setting.

© Joshua McHugh

© Bill Timmerman

This stylish, almost masculine kitchen is organized around an island of dark wood and marble. The rigorous geometry of the space is softened by organic materials such as polished stone and exposed brick, and the natural leather of the armchairs in the living area.

245

© Luuk Kramer

© Luuk Kramer

This kitchen clearly has an industrial-inspired design. Natural wood and soft white surfaces "domesticate" the space, which benefits from plenty of natural light. The L-shaped cooking/ eating arrangement is simple and practical.

© Luuk Kramer

095

In some cases, the range hood can be made into a feature, such as this L-shaped model. Natural wood (seen here in the kitchen table) can soften the coldness of stainless steel.

© Luuk Kramer

© Carlos Domínguez

096 Although it is mainly associated with commercial kitchens, stainless steel does not always look industrial, especially when combined with other elements in organic materials, such as wood or stone.

© Bill Timmerman

097

Elegant and durable polished stone makes an ideal kitchen floor. It is also surprisingly tactile and soft, and it works well with wood, brick and other organic surfaces.

© Bill Timmerman

© Stefan Meyer

This modern kitchen/service area is clearly detached from the rest of the living area in terms of both its style and placement. A change in materials, color-scheme and flooring (from hardwood to glass tile) indicates its specific function.

© Celeste Cima

253

© Sabrina Tetrao

© Sabrina Tetrao

© Ionna Roufopoulou

© Bruno Cardi, João Duaye

© Fran Parente

© Fran Parente

098 In small kitchens, try to get the most out of each unit. By using an extension of the counter top for a dining table it becomes somewhere to eat, somewhere to work, and also serves to separate the kitchen from the living area.

© Fran Parente

© Alan Gastelum

Modest and neutral, yet cosy and inviting. Every aspect of this New York apartment's design was focused on minimalism, yet it does not skimp on personality and individuality thanks to its wide variety of cohesive elements.

099 Give your kitchen a contemporary feel by installing a hydraulic mosaics floor. They are low maintenance and highly resistant, making them perfect for an area that is prone to humidity and tricky stains... Although their retro feel combines beautifully with vintage, rustic and industrial styles, they also go well with very modern kitchens.

© Carlos Domínguez

The owners have made this kitchen into the true heart of the home. It's visible from various rooms and the yard, and decorative elements, such as books, plants and even children's toys, give a warm and lived-in feel to an otherwise functional space.

© Murray Fredericks

Perfect for entertaining, this minimalist kitchen is a focal point of this home and faces the backyard and patio. Clean lines and surfaces bathed in white are in keeping with the rest of the home's stylish symmetry.

© Shania Shegedyn

This long, snakelike module is the perfect choice for the elongated, "horizontal" nature of this kitchen area, as it leaves space on either side free. The attached dining element, located in front of the glass doors that lead to the exterior, is another space-saver.

© Shania Shegedyn

© Dao Lou Zha

100 Don't discount color in the kitchen. Choices made don't need to be permanent. Brighten things up with painted feature walls (which can be changed in the future), furniture and decorative elements, such as posters.

© Eugeni Pons

© Eugeni Pons

101 This clever arrangement includes an enclosed freestanding rectangular module that contains preparation and eating areas. It also creates an extra dimension within the space. Glimpses of the adjoining rooms can be seen beyond.

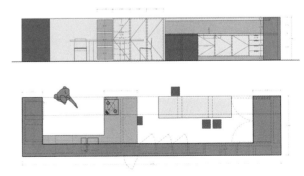

© John Gollings

© John Gollings

The most luxurious element of this kitchen is space, easily accommodating a generous freestanding cabinet in a soft yellow tone. Glass doors open out onto the yard, lending the kitchen an even greater feeling of openness, space and light.

102 You can never have too much storage space. Display only what you need day to day and put the rest in cabinets, drawers or, in this case, a walk-in pantry, located on the left.

© Bruno Klomfar

© Bruno Klomfar

White surfaces, natural wood and, above all, abundant light lend this kitchen an ethereal, floaty feel. This feeling is enhanced by a hanging sink and serving element that not only connects dining room with kitchen, but is also aesthetically pleasing.

103 Enamel paint reflects light and makes a space look larger. It is also washable and hard-wearing, making it ideal for a kitchen. It must, however, be applied to smooth, even surfaces.

104 Walls are also perfect for organizing kitchenware items, skimmers, ladles, spices and so on... Remember that if they are visible, however, as well as being functional they must not interrupt the aesthetics and harmony of the kitchen.

105

As the kitchen is one of the most used parts of the home (especially for families), it makes sense to place it where there is plenty of natural light.

© John Gollings

© John Gollings

© John Gollings

© John Gollings

A false wall (top left) shields this kitchen and can
be manipulated to let light in or to shut it out,
depending on the time of day. The dining area also
enjoys the advantages of a verdant vista through
the glass walls.

© Bruno Helbling

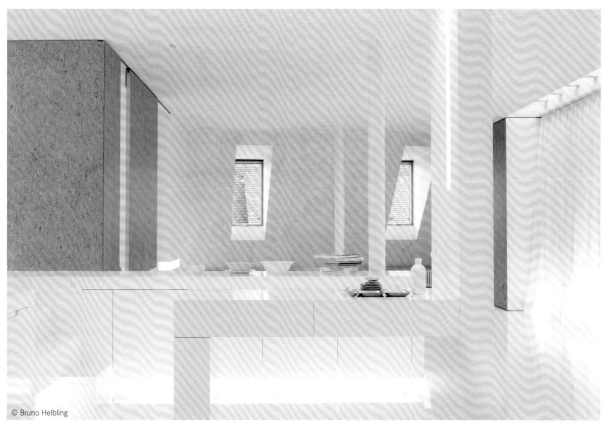

106 Lighting plays an important role in the kitchen. Angle lights so they illuminate work, eating and storage areas, and don't forget to include plenty of electrical outlets at the planning stage.

This harmonious kitchen has an abundance of elements that create different dimensions – the stepped shelving arrangement, sunken windows, columns and suspended work surface. Site-specific lighting features draw attention to the different layers.

© Andreas Llg

107 You can add warmth to an all-white
minimalist kitchen with hardwood flooring
and accessories. Here, the row of brass pots,
bird sculpture, cushions and flowers suggest
coziness and domesticity.

This Scandinavian-style kitchen is neatly fitted
into a rectangular area on the ground floor. A long
cooking/preparation module cleverly incorporates
a banquette-style dining area, avoiding the need
for a separate table and chairs.

The entrance to this stylish kitchen is clearly announced by a change in flooring and a row of kitchen utensils that hangs above the stove area on a purpose-built frame. Cabinets and doors do not have handles, creating seamless, uninterrupted surfaces.

The view is the focal point of this stylish kitchen-living room area, so furniture has been kept to an absolute minimum. The ladder-type staircase, hanging range hood and work module make a geometric composition against the backdrop of the view.

© Luuk Kramer

© Luuk Kramer

© Luuk Kramer

108 When contemplating an auxiliary kitchen, choose streamlined, discreet furniture and accessories that will not interfere with the rest of the decor. Glass-ceramic stoves are ideal.

A "dead" space below this staircase has been cleverly converted into a kitchen area. The module is away from the main wall, leaving just enough room to allow access from both sides, but close enough to it to not impose on the rest of the room.

Advances in technology and design techniques mean that installing a kitchen is now possible in almost any type of dwelling. The only real requirements are ventilation and a source of power.

The designer of this waterfront bungalow made the most of this sunken narrow space by installing an elongated counter that extends the entire length, to the upper levels of the stepped entrance. Wood decking and glossy white surfaces add to the nautical flavor.

© Luigi Filetici

© Luigi Filetici

109 Preparation areas can be discreetly defined with curtains and other vertical coverings. Here, the transparent blinds are both practical and stylish and define the space without cutting it off.

This masterful arrangement is created by the subtle tones of the textiles against the white backdrop of the kitchen area. Light and color variations are the eye-catching features, as seen in the curtains and unusual dining table.

The interplay of colors extends into the kitchen elements, as seen on the stylish range hood and "frame" around the cabinet area. The stainless steel counter reflects the chromatic scheme, and natural light from the windows enhances it.

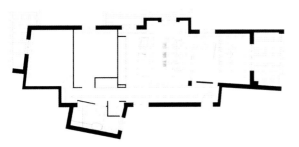

© Luigi Filetici

This tunnel-like kitchen benefits from the numerous windows and glass doors at the main entrance. The pale green panels and decorative features enhance the cool, airy ambience, while the back mirrored wall reflects the leafy exterior of the yard.

The compact arrangements on either side of this narrow kitchen have separate roles (preparation and extra seating/storage), freeing up space in the center for a dining table and chairs.

110 Large mirrors, such as the one on this back wall and the long panel above the preparation area at the far left, create the optical illusion of a much larger space. Kitchens can benefit from this as much as any other room in the home.

© Caroline Mayer

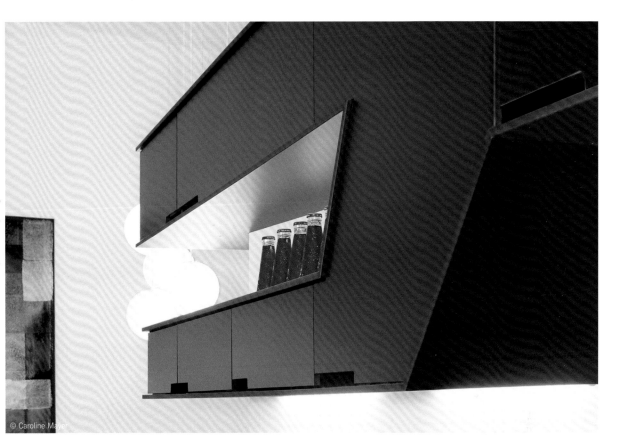

111 Think creatively if you are custom-building your kitchen. The old rules governing the design of cabinets and other modules have been broken as the kitchen becomes the prime room in the home.

© Caroline Mayer

© Caroline Mayer

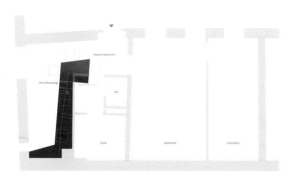

This abstract, almost aerodynamic module has been purpose-built to a highly unusual plan, providing generous preparation and cooking surfaces. The square-shaped "extension" on the lower level serves as a table, which runs along a right-angled corner.

© Caroline Mayer

© Alain Brugier

© Alain Brugier

© Murray Fredericks

This contemporary kitchen is located on an elevated floor area, clearly separating it from the living and dining areas on either side. The stove has been neatly designed into an alcove, taking advantage of the free space underneath a hanging staircase.

© Juan Solano

112

To maximise the space in an elongated, small kitchen with just one entrance, an L-shaped distribution is best.

© Francesco Di Gregorio

113 In an open-plan space, a simple color contrast can be an effective room divider without the need for furniture or any other device. Used over an immaculate white base, color can be used to define the different spaces. Here, the blacks used in the kitchen meld together as a whole and separate it from the rest of the room.

© Rogan Coles

© Rogan Coles

114 When choosing kitchen furniture, both design and functionality are key. If you do not have many cupboards, an island with drawers or storage space can be a good choice.

© Joseba Bengoetxea

115 If order, neatness and functionality are your priorities when it comes to decorating your kitchen, opt for a minimalist style: straight lines, sober colors and few decorative details. The pairing of black and white with new materials such as steel is usually the most popular.

© Taggart Sorenson

116 To break up the uniformity of your closed kitchen units, try combining them with open shelving which has a dual function – storage and decoration. Achieving a combination of order and aesthetics is not easy and you need to know how to choose elements that will be harmonious.

Air flows through the building from end to end, as does the light. The two are indispensable in this design.

© nieve, Productora Audiovisual

© Eugeni Bach

© Eugeni Bach

117 Wood reflects warmth and natural beauty. However, when used like this it can be delicate, as its appearance changes when it comes into contact with certain liquids and other elements. A waterproofing treatment would improve its lifespan.

118

It is advisable to protect your cooking area from splashes of grease and water. There are plenty of materials with which you can do this: tiles, Silestone quartz, tempered glass, steel or natural materials such as granite and marble are some of the options available.

© nieve, Productora Audiovisual

The functionality of empty spaces and straight lines can make a house's atmospheric warmth plunge below zero, but not here. The materials chosen and the use of blue serve to retain its warmth. In the intense light of day, sky blue is transformed into a warm color.

© Marco Zanta

119 Color is our greatest ally when it comes to maximizing light and space in the kitchen. To emphasize these qualities the color white should be applied to finishes and furnishing. For a classic or rustic touch, do away with the strips and laminates for modern kitchens.

120

The range of materials for kitchen designs is expanding all the time. Methacrylate gloss finish, which looks like glass, is a newly available option with many advantages. As well as offering a wide range of colors, it is easy to clean and highly resistant to impact and aging.

© Courtesy of EHTV Architectes

© Morten Odding

© Morten Odding

121   The kitchen matches with the motley decoration of the living room. The colors are inspired by the world of food: tomatoes, lemons, curry, saffron and red wine.

© Martin Tessler

122

Brick walls will not look rustic if you combine them with modern interiors. White units with clean, straight lines combined with steel stools create a very contemporary feel.

© Martin Tessler

© Jean Bourbon

© Barbara Bonomi, Gabriele Gatta

123 Eclectic style is the best way to reconcile and integrate different decorative trends in a harmonious way while also creating a homely atmosphere. Here, we have used a black marble island with pronounced veins, which transports us to the classical kitchens of yesteryear, with white lacquered modern furniture, wood flooring and an assortment of accessories of different styles and sources.

© Karina Illovska

The kitchen is integrated in the living space and open to the exterior. It is more than just a functional living area, it is a place in which to meet and celebrate.

© Federico Villa

124

Arrange your kitchen layout according to the space you have available, the different functions you need to perform and, if you have children, safety aspects. Position your dining room near a source of natural light.

© Zecc Architecten

© Karin Matz

347

© Luis da Cruz

125 Microcement is a decorative, extremely attractive and completely waterproof coating, making it an ideal material for use in the kitchen. It is a tasteful, modern alternative that is quick to install and easy to maintain. It is a versatile material that provides absolute freedom in design execution and combines easily with other materials. With no joins, it also adds a feeling of continuity to spaces.

351

© Eduardo Girão

© Eduardo Girão

© Costa Picadas

© Costa Picadas

126 Accessories such as faucets, lights and other elements are transformed into decorative elements if they are chosen and positioned in a certain way. Choose a good design for optimum effect.

© Marc Mormeneo

127 The pine wood wall panels conceal all the kitchen's appliances and provide generous storage space, contributing to the clean look of the kitchen. The hood integrates open shelving, offering easy access to items that are used daily.

© 3mille

128

There are many advantages to using stainless steel furniture in the kitchen: it is strong, easy to maintain, safe – as it does not contaminate food in any way – and, lastly, it coordinates very easily with other materials. In this kitchen the large appliances are integrated so as to be barely visible, creating a very interesting urban industrial aesthetic.

© Laurent Saint Jean, 3MILLE

© Vassilis Makris

© Vassilis Makris

129 Independent modules create spaces within other spaces and can add volume even in the smallest kitchen. The classical approach of fixing kitchen furniture to the walls is no longer the only option.

© Santi Caleca

130

Hard-wearing, versatile and mobile outdoor furniture can often make ideal kitchen furniture. If your kitchen has access to the outside, chairs, tables and benches can be used in both areas.

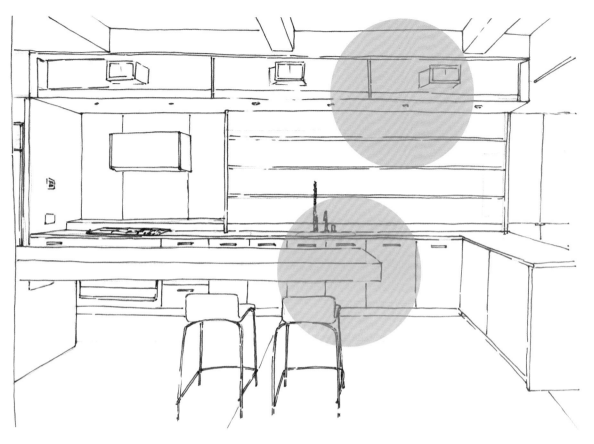

131 When there is limited space for a the dining table, try to integrate it into the kitchen fixtures. Placing a counter close to the cooking area is a practical idea for breakfasts or a quick lunch. Another alternative in small spaces is a folding table.

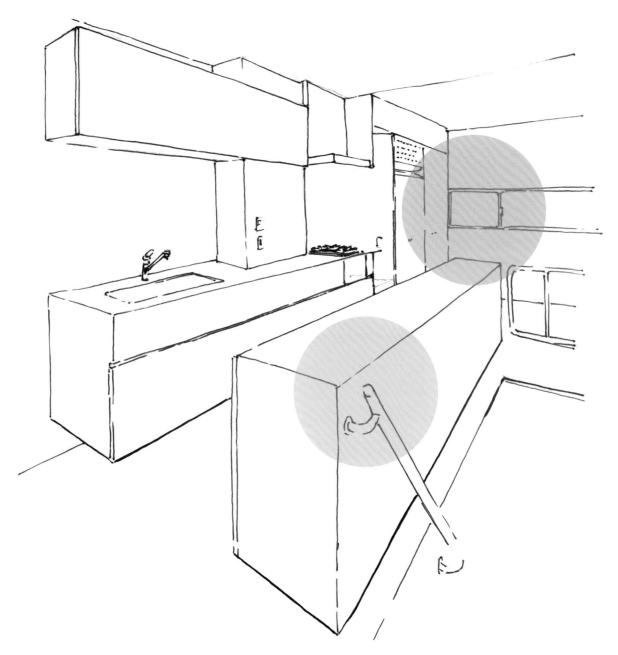

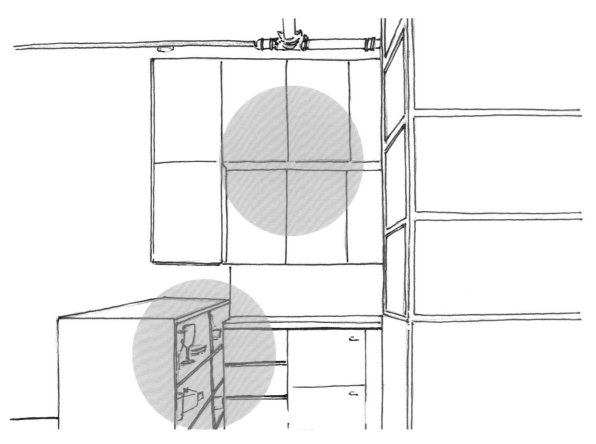

132 Good ventilation is important in the kitchen. High-quality windows are also more secure and provide better thermal insulation. There are a multitude of different kinds available, which combine technology and design. It is also advisable to install versatile furniture that incorporates plenty of storage.

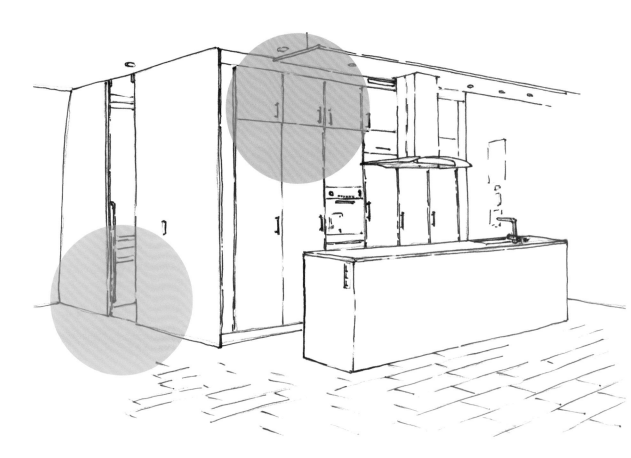

133 The type of ceiling will determine the best lighting system for the kitchen, where halogen bulbs are generally the best choice. If the ceiling is low, pot lights — round or square halogen lights that are set into the ceiling — are a good option.

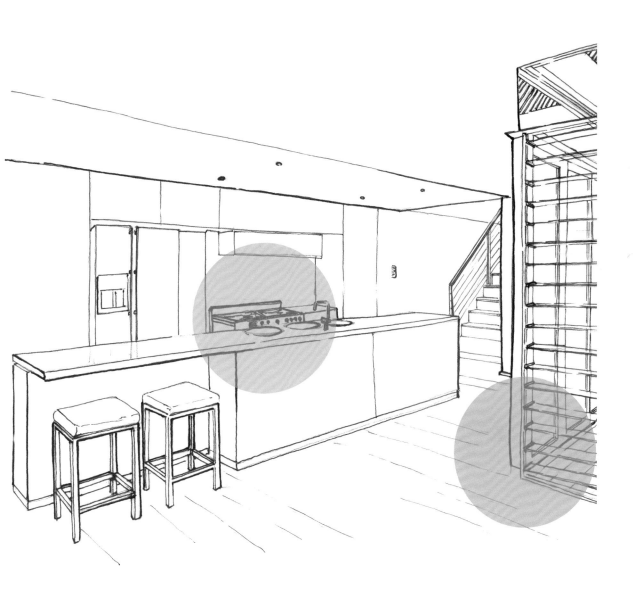

BEDROOMS

We spend about a third of our lives sleeping. Given this, and the other customs we perform in our bedroom, it's safe to say that, along with the bathroom, the bedroom is the most personal space in the home.

Bedrooms can be large or small and located in an attic, underneath a staircase, or almost anywhere. The main rule is that they should be in the quietest area of the home, as far away from the noise that kitchens, bathrooms and hallways produce. Naturally, the most important element is the bed, which should be chosen for comfort (which varies from person to person) and according to the space you have available.

Although the tendency these days is for oversized king and queen beds, you should only choose one of these if you have sufficient space. Your bed needs to "breathe," and a good night's sleep is rarely had with four walls closing in on you or under a canopy that takes over the room. Likewise, closet and armoire doors need to open and close easily, without bumping into the bed or other furniture.

It is difficult to overestimate the amount of closet space you will need. Remember, it will not only be used for clothing, shoes and accessories, but you may also need to store spare bed linen, blankets and so many other things in it. Built-in closets work best, or choose shelving and racks that can be hidden by drapes, screens or blinds. Many manufacturers produce attractive "expandable" closets and storage units that can be added to as needed. Extra storage space can also be found underneath the bed. Look for boxes and drawers that will fit neatly into the space under your bed, or choose a bed that has a built-in storage system. Whatever you choose, make sure it is well lit. Specific lighting devices for storage areas are now widely available.

In terms of color, it is generally accepted that neutral or pastel shades promote a sense of tranquility and rest. Stick to these shades unless you want to make a particular statement. Of course, color can be used, especially in the choice of bed linen. Nothing works quite as well as a colorful throw or bedspread lying against crisp white cotton sheets. Load your bed with extra cushions and other objects (such as fluffy toys) with the utmost restraint: nobody wants to spend time "unmaking" their bed when they are tired.

Soft floor coverings create a comfortable, warm ambiance and absorb noise. If you prefer hardwood floors, place a small rug at the side of your bed – the first thing your feet touch when you get up. Natural light can enhance a bedroom greatly, but choose a covering, be it drapes or a blind, that blocks out daylight. Venetian blinds allow us to manipulate light, so we can let in as much or little as we want. To a lesser degree, the same can be done with drapes by using a heavy insulating lining together with a more transparent, floaty fabric on top.

Good bedside lighting will encourage you to read in bed. An extra burst of light can come from a standing lamp or even a floor lamp. Recessed lighting (a light source "hidden" in the ceiling or wall, such as pot lights) can also create moods, and a pair of wall-mounted lamps work well when placed on either side of the headboard.

Modern life dictates that the bedroom is not just used for sleeping. Many people like to watch television and use other forms of home entertainment in bed. Fortunately, stylish and attractive systems that allow you to do this are available for most budgets.

Work spaces are also often incorporated into bedrooms, either in the form of a custom-built surface or a freestanding desk. If you plan to do this, position the desk or work surface next to the room's source of natural light.

Children's bedrooms offer far more opportunity for creativity, be it a special play area, a fantasy bed, mobiles, feature walls or other accessories. But remember that children grow up quickly, and at some point they are going to want to personalize their bedrooms themselves, so any renovations should not be too permanent. In this respect, decorating your child's room with colorful wallpaper can be a good idea.

The traditional dressing table is now a thing of the past, as the modern woman tends to keep her beauty products and makeup in the bathroom, not having time to sit down and preen in front of a mirror for too long. That said, there should be a small shelf or unit in the bedroom for perfumes, jewelry and other personal objects. Items that are frequently "on show", such as slippers and bathrobes, can be chosen to match your bed linen. A good mirror, preferably full length, is essential in the bedroom, and it will quickly become the last thing you look at before leaving the room.

375

© Tim Van de Velde

134 Choosing multifunctional furniture is a hit in any small space. Here, the headboard doubles as a worktable and, by placing it behind the bookcase, the two spaces are perfectly defined without any physical separation.

© hoo

135

When choosing a headboard for a small bedroom forget about large and heavy structures, as they will overfill the space. Using a light shade will also lighten up the room.

© Conran & Partners

This urban apartment is blessed with spectacular views. The sleeping and working areas take full advantage of them, whereas living, cooking and bathing take place in the back of the home.

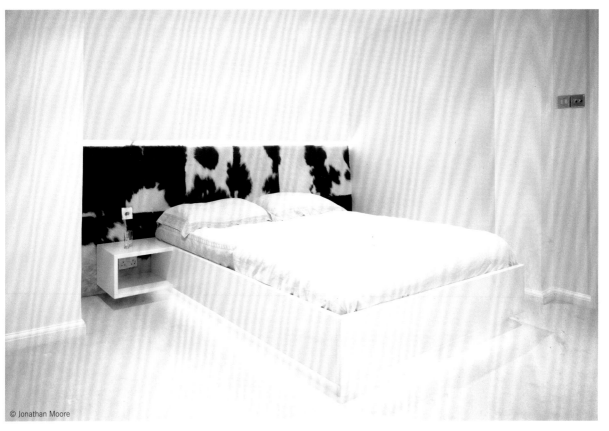

© Jonathan Moore

This custom-made bed base incorporates modular bedside tables. The separate headboard, covered in calfskin, is a dramatic counterpoint to the white linen and wood. The recessed lighting elements that frame the headboard and the bed's base add depth.

136

Every bedroom needs a bedside or accent table next to the bed for books, a lamp and other objects. Headboards can add depth and color, and they can even incorporate a lighting feature. A freestanding headboard is easier to personalize.

© Taggart Sorenson

137 The bed is the centrepiece on which the entire decor hangs. Therefore, before buying, calculate how much room will be left for bedside tables on either side. If it is a large bedroom, you can add a bench at the foot of the bed and for leaving cushions on at night. With regard to the orientation, aim to locate the headboard next to the window so that the natural light does not bother you.

© Eduardo Girão

© Eduardo Girão

138 When it comes to decorating your bedroom, use wall hangings or wallpaper on the wall on which the bed is to be positioned in order to mark it out from the rest of the room and give it a more distinguished feel. An easier-to-maintain, equivalent decorative alternative is wood panelling.

139 The placement and angle of your bed are important, and many believe they can even affect the quality of your sleep. Position your bed to enjoy views and natural light.

© Paul Smoothy

Here, different areas within a loft-type space have been created using a single custom-built element. On one side it accommodates a home entertainment system, and on the other side there is storage for clothes and a wall that encloses the sleeping area.

© Tony Miller

© Tony Miller

Various spaces within this unusual oval-shaped apartment have been created with interior right-angled walls. A harmonious color scheme of grape, slate and taupe has been used throughout, including the bedroom.

© Stefano Graziani

© Luis da Cruz

140

Localized lighting is important. Whether they are next to the bed or above it, lamps should not cast shadows, as this will impede your ability to read. It is also important that you can easily control the lights from the comfort of your bed.

© Jan Bitter

141 Vertical or venetian blinds are an attractive
option for dressing large windows as they
enable you to control both the visibility and
the amount of sunlight that you want to let
in at any given time, simply by changing the
angle of the slats. There are a huge variety
of materials and designs with which they
can be made, offering a wide spectrum of
decorative options.

© Adam Butler

142 Bedrooms offer a good opportunity to play with textures; experiment with bed linen, cushions and drapes. Rugs are particularly important around the bed area.

This eclectic bedroom draws its inspiration from mid-1970s decor. The hanging chair is both fun and useful, whereas the artwork and warm neutral tones keep the composition contemporary and prevent it from falling into the trap of kitsch.

© Sabrina Tetrao

© Sabrina Tetrao

143 Gray is one of the key colours in contemporary interior design. Many consider it to be the "new white" because of its versatility, although it also adds a slightly more modern and sober touch to rooms with which we decorate it.

144   The furniture is composed of simple and elegant lines, and the color range adds warmth to the different spaces.

© Luis Ros

This bedroom, which is adjacent to a terrace, can be opened up on warm evenings. Seductive lighting creates a mysterious air at night and enhances the yard. Hardwood floors and walls add to the inside/outside ambiance.

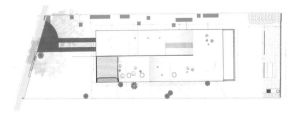

© Luis Ros

© Satoshi Asakawa

145 Whether minimalist or more elaborate, your bedroom is your very own private sanctuary. Use slippers, robes and other items to heighten its ritualistic role in the home.

Although this design is heavily influenced by a traditional Japanese bedroom, a more conventional Western-style bed has been chosen, instead of a futon. The retractable panel-type flooring can create different levels within the room.

146 The bed is the most important investment in a bedroom. Choose a good base and a good mattress. Latex and memory foam are best for fitting to the body. Before deciding, test it out with a pillow.

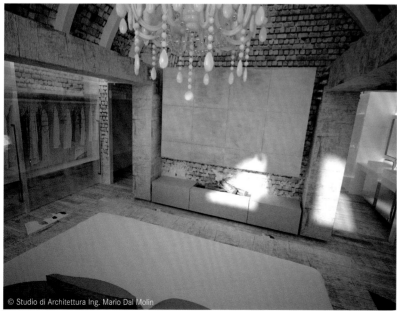

147 Because bedrooms are a place to rest, the use of color in them should be restrained. It is best to use colors in bedspreads, throws and cushions, as they can be changed to suit the mood. Avoid bold colors on the walls.

© Olivier Hallot

148 Attic bedrooms are particularly warm and alluring. Place your bed underneath the skylight, which should be covered with made-to-measure drapes or blinds that are easy to open.

149 A terrace can be transformed into an extension of a bedroom. Place comfortable loungers on it and a table at which you can eat breakfast, lunch or dinner in privacy, ensuring that the style remains in keeping with the interior decor and the harmony of your bedroom space.

© Donna Griffith

150 Like silk, velvet has always been considered a luxury fabric, as it is quite complex to produce. Using velvet for the headboard not only feels pleasant but it also creates a feeling of sophistication and elegance.

© Oksana Perkins

© Véronique Mati

151 To create maximum warmth in a room choose hardwood or laminated wood floors and dress them with wool rugs or skins that envelop your feet when you take your shoes off.

© Vangelis Paterakis

152 A monochrome palette, recycled objects and wooden highlights lend a feeling of elegant warmth and simplicity to the space.

© André Nazareth, João Duayer

153 Opting for intimate decor full of memories and trinkets creates an incredible effect in a bedroom, conveying the sense of a cosy and lived-in environment.

© Vassilis Makris

© Ondrej Synak

154 The stairs are cut on a zigzag, like all the lines of this house. Suggestive ideas are found not only in the walls and furnishings, but even in the steps.

© Livio Marrese

155 The canopy is an ornament that was used historically, a classic that never dies and has indeed evolved. A bedroom with a canopy evokes a romantic feel, creating a warm, pleasant and tranquil atmosphere. However, before installing one in your bedroom do take note of the ceiling height and square meters available: they are not a good idea if the ceiling is low or the room small.

156

A bedroom attached to an en-suite bathroom is a reality in many of today's homes. There are various solutions to ensure this connection is both harmonious and practical: to gain privacy without losing the visual continuity, a half-height wall, one that is open on both sides, carefully chosen furniture such as the bedhead or a wardrobe are all good options. And there is more: try to establish a passage between the two areas, such as a step that positions them at different heights or using glass as an element of separation-integration.

© Vincent van den Hoven

423

© Ionna Roufopoulou

© Héctor Santos-Díez, BISimages

157 To give your bedroom an original and more functional feel, a small headboard integrated into a custom unit with shelves included is a good option that will be both attractive and practical.

© Gianni Franchellucci

© Bruno Cardi, João Duaye

158

Like mattress and pillow, bed linen plays an important role in guaranteeing a good night's sleep. When choosing, seek comfort and beauty but also think about your health. Always use 100% cotton sheets and duvet covers. These provide natural ventilation as they allow you to perspire and do not retain moisture.

© Victor Hugo, Mauricio Fuertes

© Carola Ripamonti

© Carola Ripamonti

© Carola Ripamonti

433

© Carola Ripamonti, Stefano Graziani

The architects designed the furnishings. They may be recycled but they are new ideas. Repainting old furniture is one thing, but giving it a completely new function within the house is quite another.

© Vladislav Kostadinov

Speaking of ingenuity: the entire floor is made of wood. The black and white grain is painted on top. The diagonals add width to this over-long house.

© João Morgado – Architecture Photography

159 Large cushions can also form a fluffy headboard and have the added advantage of offering plenty of support for the neck. Try not to clutter the bed with too many pillows and small decorative cushions.

445

160

It is proven that light colors such as whites and creams help us to sleep better. Furthermore, white should be your first choice if you are decorating a small room. The ideal is to paint the walls in this color so as to maximise light, clarity and a sense of spaciousness, adding splashes of color with decorative elements.

© Marcin Ratajczak

161   If you have enough space, when decorating a
child's room try to create three distinct areas
for sleeping, playing and studying.

162   Storage space is essential in a child's bedroom and, if possible, some of this should be at the child's height in order to teach them how to organize their belongings while freeing up space for playing and learning.

© John Sinal

450

163

Personalizing a bedroom can be fun and easy. Murals, collages, soft objects and even graffiti can all be used to make feature walls with flair, especially in children's bedrooms.

© John Sinal

164 Fine materials such as wood, environmentally
friendly paints, natural fabrics, natural light
and ventilation will make your child's room a
healthy space.

455

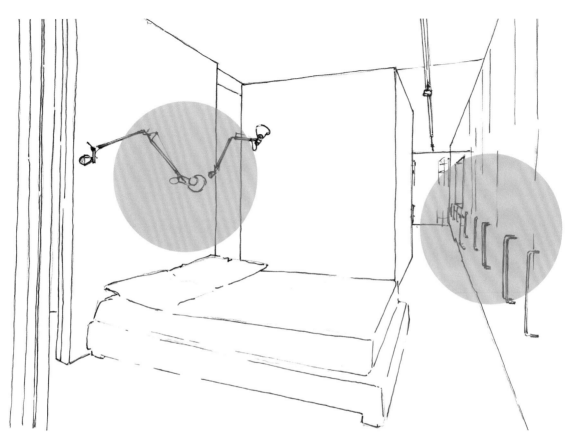

165 Storing clothes requires good organization, with rods, shelves and drawers that make it easy to find articles and accessories quickly. Lighting in the bedroom will depend on the size of the room and the color of the walls.

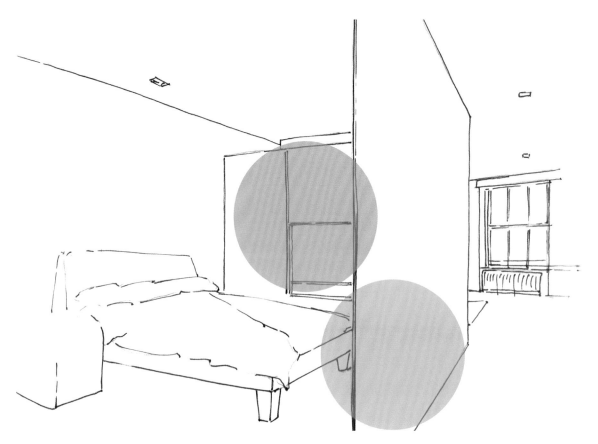

166 When creating a suite – with a bedroom, bathroom and small living area – you must take the dimensions of the room into account. Use a dividing panel to separate the bedroom without affecting the visual fluidity between the spaces.

167 Separating spaces with movable partition walls allows you to adapt your house to changing needs. This is a good solution for small apartments, making it possible to turn two or three rooms into just one.

BATHROOMS

The concept of the bathroom has been revolutionized over the past decade. A culture of well-being and a proliferation of day spas have led many designers to transfer these principles to the domestic sphere. Although its use remains mostly functional, the bathroom is not merely a space to carry out our daily ablutions. Scandinavian, Japanese and Arabic cultures have known this for centuries. In these countries, the bathroom is considered an important space in the home, and it is given as much space and attention to detail as any other domestic area.

In cultures where the bathroom's purpose is not merely functional, large bathtubs often figure prominently, and they are used for long periods, for relaxing and regaining a sense of well-being. They cater to all of the senses, using essential oils in saunas, the texture of natural stone in Japanese bathrooms and candles and fresh flowers in Arabic bathhouses. As these trends hit the rest of the world, designers and interior architects started to rethink the sanitary, "hygienic" aesthetic that had long been associated with bathrooms. One need only to look at Jaime Hayon's brightly colored neo-baroque vanity basins, baths and mirrors for the Spanish firm ArtQuitect or Ross Lovegrove's voluminous oval bath tubs for Vitra.

Technology, of course, has also had a part to play. Domestic massage showers, Jacuzzis, saunas and other water therapy devices are now widely available. In terms of designs, new, more functional and more readily available materials mean that the bathroom can be as personalized as any other a space.

Bathrooms can now be conceived in an endless variety of materials. Marble is still dominant, especially for elegant bathrooms (the term "marble bathroom" is still part of the luxury hotel lexicon).

Although glass and stone have made advances, it is hard to imagine they will ever surpass the practicality of ceramic sinks and tubs. Wood adds warmth, although a variety with a high oil content (such as teak) should be used, as they are more resistant to water. Small glass mosaic tiles add color and texture and can be used to cover an entire space (such as a floor or wall) or as a "feature" (for example, covering the exterior of a bathtub). Metals and plastic resins are all water-resistant and are increasingly used in modern bathroom design because of their flexibility and value for money. Even water-resistant

paints, when properly applied, can provide colorful low-cost surfaces and will wear well if your bathroom has adequate ventilation.

The global village has also influenecd bathroom design, with "tadelakt" and stucco from hammams (public bathhouses in Arabic countries), slate from Japan and natural wood from northern Europe. Decoration and accessories, once seen as superfluous, now adorn most bathrooms. Bottles for products, water-resistant lamps, mirrors and other elements can be matched (or mismatched) to the decor, creating an eclectic visual theme.

Despite this diversity, modern bathroom (or any room) decor can be categorized into two principal schools. Minimalism is still at the forefront of modern bathroom interiors, where less is more, except when it comes to the main elements: light and space. Minimalist bathrooms are generally executed in white ceramic (for the fixtures), with glass, marble and steel for the accessories and other elements, such as the floor and partitions. Lines are clean and the space is free of adornment. This style is more suited to single people and couples, as the clutter associated with family bathrooms is at odds with the dictum's principal aesthetic. Towels and other bathroom items are stored in built-in cabinets and drawers, so as not to interfere with the bathroom's right-angled symmetry.

The opposite of minimalism, of course, is maximalism, and this has been the biggest revolution in contemporary bathroom design. Maximalist spaces are loud and proud, with bold color, metallic finishes and rounded forms. They often take inspiration from florid 18th- and 19th-century interiors (or at least the reinterpretation of these styles, as seen in the neo-Baroque interior trends of the 1960s and 1970s). Maximalism offers more scope in terms of eclecticism and personalization. Feel like putting a gilt-edged mirror above the sink? Why not? You can rest a Murano glass water jug on the edge of the bathtub or cover the window with that piece of vintage Marimekko fabric you have been wanting to use.

Of course, between these two poles there are a myriad of variations. Explore the limits of the space you are working with, your budget and, most importantly, your imagination to make your bathrooms your personal retreat.

© Juan Rodriguez

465

© Carola Ripamonti

© Carola Ripamonti

467

469

168

A Zen-like tranquility can be achieved by using natural stone and a minimal color palette. Keep products out of sight or decant them into vessels made of organic materials.

© Fabien Baron

169

If space permits, a double sink is the ideal in large houses. Here, we have also taken advantage of all the space beneath to locate a large-capacity suspended cupboard so as to remove the majority of products from view and give a sense of order.

© Fran Parente

473

170

Install a jacuzzi bath to provide relaxation and well-being, so coveted by stressed-out city dwellers. Bearing in mind the shape of your bathroom, you can choose the bathtub that best meets your taste and space, but do note the capacity of your hot-water heater and the size of the bath, so you can be sure you will be able to fill your tub with hot water

© Joerg Springer, Robert Mieth

© Joerg Springer, Robert Mieth

© Joerg Springer, Robert Mieth

© Virginia Del Giudice

171 Minimalism need not be cold. Here, a period piece of furniture and other traditional elements have been placed among modern steel shelves and fixtures, creating a juxtaposition of old and new.

This bathroom is in a purpose-built unit and is the focal point of the sleeping and dressing area of the home. The swiveling mirror and open-sided walls ensure constant dialogue with the rest of the area – the antithesis of the historical "closed off" bathroom.

© Alfonso Postigo

172 Long, narrow bathrooms can benefit from large mirrors and keeping materials and finishes to an absolute minimum. Note the elongated sink, which is in keeping with the rest of the room's proportions.

© Alfonso Postigo

© Alfonso Postigo

This visually clean bathroom makes the most of the space's awkward geometry by keeping cabinets, faucets and fixtures flush and fitted. An unusual walk-in sunken bath-shower is this bathroom's most personal element.

The architects of this home placed the bathroom in a purpose-built pod that is supported by angled metal rods from the ground floor. The glass wall and the pod's position lend a voyeuristic tone to the element.

© Andrea Martiradonna

481

An Arabic-bathhouse influence can be seen in this striking bathroom. Turquoise tiles cover every surface, from the oversized screen-less shower to the sunken sink. The scarlet-red door frames the space and adds drama.

© Carlos Domínguez

© Carlos Domínguez

This highly personalized bathroom has been rendered in several shades of purple, from the toilet and bidet to the faucets and products. The fluid platinum and white vanity unit and counter define the space and connect it with the ceiling and wall decorations.

173 Don't be confined to traditional thinking when it comes to your bathroom. An endless variety of colors, forms and textures are all possible, using new techniques in laminates, metal and plastic.

© Angelo Kaunat

174 In loft-type dwellings, consider sectioning off the bathroom area with a screen or freestanding partition. An articulated screen can provide space for storage units and shelving on the inside, and it can also be manipulated so the bathroom becomes fully integrated into the home.

© Jordi Canosa

© Duravit

© Duravit

© Duravit

175 Freestanding bathroom furniture, such as the vanity unit above, can make a bathroom feel more spacious. The glass partitions and walls define the room without boxing in the different areas.

Bold color, uncluttered forms, geometry and decorative elements mark this spectacular contemporary bathroom. The addition of art and books takes the emphasis away from daily ablutions and converts the space into one of contemplation and learning.

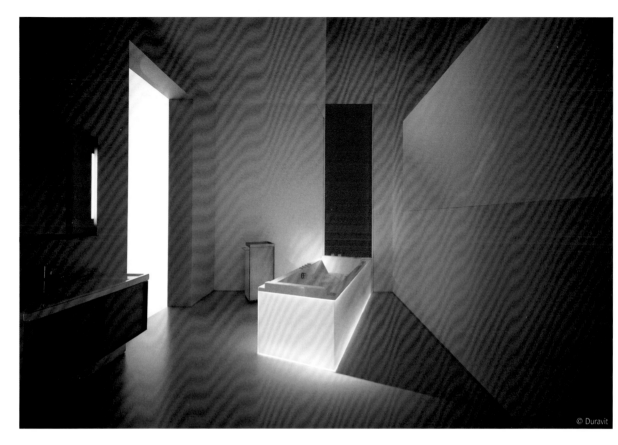

© Duravit

This high-tech bathroom has been designed on the principles of chromo-therapy, or the use of colored lights to balance and promote well-being. In this case, pink stimulates sensitivity, purple evokes spirituality and contemplation whereas red is the color of emotions.

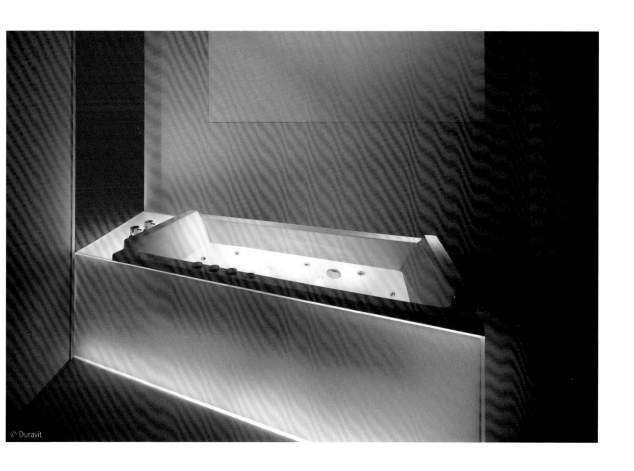

© Hiroyuki Hirai

This arc-shaped bathtub has been placed outdoors, overlooking a spectacular natural vista. With water shortages becoming acute and green principles taking hold, architects have taken the concept of outdoor tubs to rural hotel suites, replacing the need for a communal pool.

© Hiroyuki Hirai

491

© Daici Ano

© Daici ano

© Daici Ano

176 There is a second bathroom on the mezzanine floor of this industrial-inspired loft-type home. It is kept free of adornment and furniture, heightening the purely functional role of the bathroom's elements, such as the sink and tub.

495

© Ionna Roufopoulou

© Sabrina Tetrao

177 The bathroom needs general lighting that is as close as possible to natural light, as well as focused or directional lighting on specific areas. The lighting over the sink and toilet should be uniform, creating no shadows or reflections.

© Sabrina Tetrao

© Sabrina Tetrao

© Vassilis Makris

The contemporary design uses natural materials (travertine and wood) and bold gray paint, all softened by natural light and contrasted with the LED illumination set.

178 Hanging shelves in the bathroom can perform two roles: they can be decorative, as a place in which to display objects that add character to the room, and they can be functional. Use wicker baskets or boxes to keep products out of sight.

© Federico Villa

© Maurizio Marcato

The walls of this dramatic bathroom are covered in tiny glass mosaic tiles – a huge trend in bathroom decor in recent years. The composition of linear furniture and bold colors is reminiscent of an abstract painting.

© Maurizio Marcato

© Eric Laignel

© Tom Ross of Brilliant Creek

179 For an elegant and contemporary finish that will not quickly become outdated, ceramic mosaic tiling is a wise choice. Tiles are highly resistant to physical and chemical extremes, as well as being very versatile and easy to clean.

180

In small bathrooms mirrors are essential, not only for looking at ourselves but also for enhancing the light and giving a greater feeling of space. For this reason, try to go for large, frame-free formats.

Marcin Ratajczak

© Laziz Hamani

181   We can make our bathroom stand out by
highlighting one of the utilities as its main
feature. This is a good example of how a
bathtub can transform the bathroom into
a very special place.

© Estudio Teresa Sapey

© Estudio Teresa Sapey

© Ross Honeysett

© Juan David Fuertes Fotografía

© Juan David Fuertes Fotografía

© Estudi EPDSE

518

182

When it comes to choosing finishes for small spaces, gentle colors without much contrast are best. If you like white, this is the best option for creating a sense of space. Do be open to the possibilities of new materials, too, such as wallpaper.

© Víctor Hugo, Mauricio Fuertes

183

In addition to its aesthetic charm, decorating a bathroom in vintage style has the advantage of never going out of fashion. The pedestal sink, taps, flooring and wall cladding all serve to create this vintage yet refined effect. Add accessories such as soap dishes, pots, brass buckets and so on to help to create this style.

© Alan Gastelum

© i29 | Interior Architects

184 Screens can help to create more space. If we use transparent ones they do not break up the visual effect of the room.

© Jan Bitter

© Joy Von Tiedemann

185 Our concept of "modesty" has changed greatly over the past decades, especially in the built-up suburbs. Opening up bathrooms to the rest of the home with glass partitions provides light and space, which is often preferred over privacy.

This mezzanine-floor bathroom has the same warm Scandinavian decor as the bedroom. Although there is a separate entrance via a hallway, divisions are lost through the use of a glass partition, which, when fully opened, integrates the bathroom into the bedroom.

© Davide Arena

© Tim Griffith

186

Depending on the level of privacy you want, you can do away with the need to close the shower area, freeing up a lot of space in turn. However, do ensure the showerhead and drain are correctly positioned in order to avoid flooding or dampening of your bathroom products and accessories.

© Bart Michiels, Robert Garneau

535

Not just minimal and space saving, it has the glamour of a batcave or a James Bond movie.

© Charles Hosea, Mike Neale

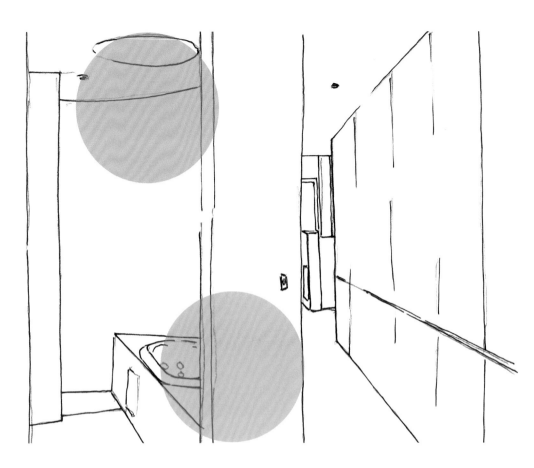

187   There are currently an infinite number
of avant-garde solutions for bathrooms.
Companies have devised ingenious methods
for installing bathroom fixtures and
accessories — including pieces by prestigious
designers — that can adapt to any space.

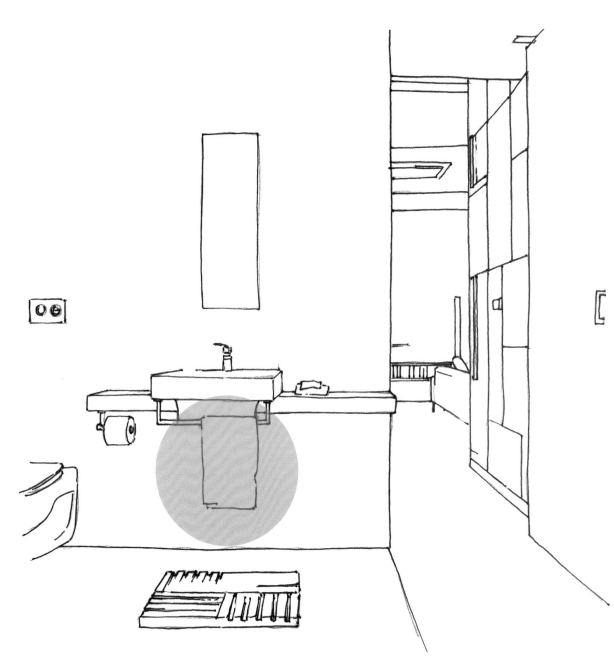

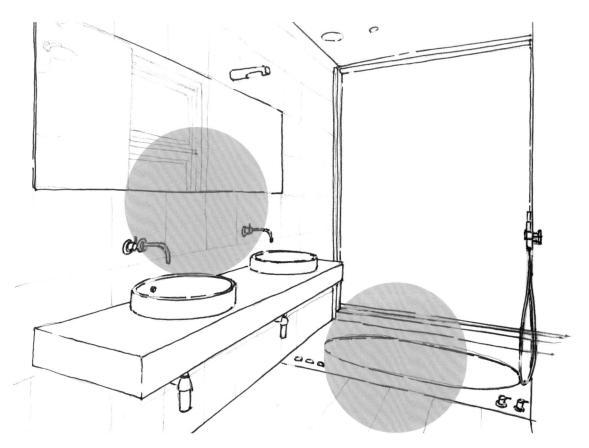

188 Simple, natural geometry characterizes the modern bathroom, where relaxation and harmonious style prevail. Innovative bathroom fixtures enable enjoyment of a bath as never before, with single- or double-handle faucets on simple or double ceramic mounts, which adapt to the size of the tub.

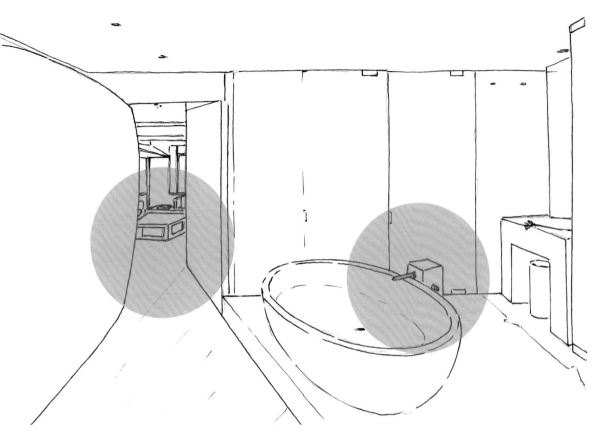

189   Today bathrooms can be turned into authentic home spas by installing comfortable bathtubs and hydrotherapy systems. There are acrylic, cast iron and steel tubs in sizes, colors and shapes to suit all tastes. Bathrooms are now equipped with everything necessary to relax and achieve a feeling of well-being.

OUTSIDE SPACES

As societies have become increasingly urbanized, our contact with Mother Nature has diminished. Yards and gardens are generally only found in the suburbs, belonging to homes with plenty of space, more than three bedrooms and picket fences. For urban dwellers, and those who live in congested "vertical" cities such as New York, Mumbai and Barcelona, the terrace or deck became an ideal solution.

Only a few are lucky enough to have a terrace or deck, and they generally pay more for the privilege. Newly built constructions usually work them into the design, or at least provide a generous balcony. Often, people who do have outside space don't use it to its full advantage; balconies are frequently neglected and decks and terraces are filled with little-used junk. Try to avoid cluttering up your outdoor area by installing some type of storage element in order to take full advantage of your deck lifestyle.

The common myth used to be that terraces were only suitable in hot climates. Recent advances in outdoor heating have proved this wrong. If you live in a chillier climate, explore options such as infrared "umbrella" heaters, gas spot heaters and even coal heaters. Lighting can also provide warmth. Outdoor lighting can be stylish as well as practical. Cleverly positioned partitions provide protection from gusts of wind and canopies can offer further shelter.

When it comes to choosing materials for your deck, the guiding principle is to keep them natural. Wood, stone and bamboo can be made into nearly every element you need. The exceptions are Plexiglas and, in some cases, glass, both of which enhance a feeling of uninterrupted space and easily adapt to most dimensions.

In terms of decoration, keep it minimal. Remember that whatever you put outdoors will be exposed to the elements, and carting a bunch of cushions inside or taking down drapery in wet weather will discourage you from using your deck. Candles, plants in pretty pots and permanent fixtures, such as a tiled wall or water feature, can generally provide all the visual attractions you crave, and the rest will be supplied by Mother Nature herself in the views — be they verdant or urban — that your deck provides.

One major mistake we often make is considering our outdoor area too small to be useful. A bit of careful planning and imagination will reveal that this is not the case. Even if your balcony only has room for a cushion, you will be amazed at just how often you end up sitting on it, either reading a book or simply watching the world go by. Plant a herb garden and watch it grow, enjoying the fragrant aromas that waft through your apartment.

If you do have the advantage of space, put as much attention into your deck as you would into any other area of your home. Install an outdoor barbecue and food preparation area. A private pool or Jacuzzi is the ultimate in luxury, but take the cost and constant maintenance requirements into consideration. If you think you will be eating outdoors regularly, choose a comfortable dining suite and protect it with a canopy, thus keeping your carefully planned dinner party from having to decamp indoors at the last minute. If you like gardening, install plenty of plants. If not, go for low-maintenance varieties, although remote and time-controlled watering systems can do the work for you. Try to install elements that respond to the landscape beyond, be it a hedge, a wall that echoes the shape of a distant building or a piece of furniture that complements the surrounding architecture. If stuck for ideas, hire a professional landscape gardener: you will be amazed at how the right choice of foliage, benches and other elements can enhance your outdoor space.

If you are remodeling your home, and your deck or terrace, try not to cut this space off from the interior. If possible, widen the entrance to it using glass doors that retract easily. Incorporate the same colors and/or materials as the area that leads to your deck or terrace, ensuring a continuous flow of space. If your deck or terrace is sunken, embellish the stairs or walkway to it with organic features and site-specific lighting, thus giving it prominence. Keep deck enclosures freshly painted and clean. However small, cut off, misshapen or dark your outdoor space is, lavish time and attention on it. In increasingly built-up areas they are our true personal oasis, our haven in which to escape the bustling world beyond.

547

190

Create privacy on urban decks with partition walls and elevated elements. Here, the undulated, built-in lounge chairs act as both furniture and screens, protecting the rest of the terrace from curious eyes. More easily manipulated than most coverings, wooden decking is the ideal material for installations of this nature.

© David Joseph

This deck has unusual angles and varying heights in the different elements, creating an avant-garde composition. Rows of wood-deck "aisles" clad the floor, which is elevated at one end, where foliage has been planted.

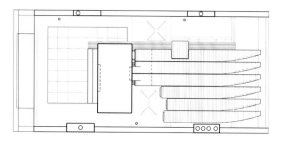

A long, narrow deck adds an extra dimension to this residence. The blood-red horizontal feature wall incorporates the deck into the rest of the home and accentuates the length of the deck.

191

Entertaining outdoors requires the same amenities as entertaining indoors: a sink and preparation area, cooking facilities and comfortable, stylish furniture. Here, the entertaining and pool areas have been defined by different levels.

© Raimund Koch

© Raimund Koch

© Raimund Koch

Different woods have been used to create a spectacular outdoor living area. Half-enclosed rooms and varying levels define the different functions, from pool to changing room to cooking area.

© Raimund Koch

192

Acrylic fencing and partitions make ideal, safe and contemporary deck and balcony enclosures. You will enjoy uninterrupted views, and the materials are flexible and lend themselves to most designs. Colors and tints can be added to the material.

© Patrick Wong

© Patrick Wong

557

© Ger Van Der Vlugt

© Ger Van Der Vlugt

193 Even very small balconies can create an outdoor "room." Choose folding furniture that can be stored when not in use, and look for vertical shelving for plants and other objects. A balcony is not a storage room; keep clutter away, as it will discourage use of the space.

These boxlike balconies have been given a new dimension by enclosing them in color-tinted acrylic walls. The underside of the floors are also colored, creating a Mondrian-like effect over the facade of the building.

This chic deck, overlooking a marina, is fully integrated into the home via folding glass doors. The metal railing is in keeping with the modernist industrial architecture.

© David Hecht/Tannerhecht

© Oscar Necoechea

194 Polished stone tiles and ceramics are ideal for terrace floors, especially if they are very exposed to the elements, as they are highly resistant.

Long, narrow decks have been designed around this home's main volume. A mirrored wall gives the illusion of space, and unusual cross-shaped supporting columns create a dramatic geometric composition.

© Oscar Necoechea

© Arnaldo Papalardo

This simple, serene enclosed deck has been
executed in natural yet sophisticated materials.
The false bamboo ceiling is backlit, letting
diffused light trickle over the entire space.

195

Remember to bear in mind climatic conditions when it comes to choosing your terrace furniture. Once it is in place it needs to withstand the elements and the test of time. The best materials to use are teak, synthetic rattan, resin and wrought iron. Materials such as steel and aluminium are also a good option as long as they are treated to avoid them deteriorating.

© Daniel Levin

© Dean Bradley

It was particularly important for the designers to consider how to fence the pool without it being offensive to the entertaining area outside of the pool space.

196   There are many advantages to installing
a natural wood floor: a warm and highly
attractive finish, strength and durability, a
wide range of colors and finishes, the ability
to conceal drainage features and last but not
least, versatility. They can be installed over
any surface and be used to create different
elements such as planters, furniture, storage
areas, or fully integrated spaces. The only
drawback is that it needs to be treated with
a nourishing oil once or twice a year.

© Zeco Architecten

© Chris Ott

This expansive apartment deck enjoys a privileged coastal view, unhindered thanks to the glass safety wall. Decked in hard-wearing red cedar, the nautical blue wall defines the space and creates a connection with the sea.

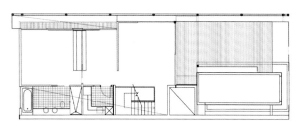

© Ross Honeysett

© Central de arquitectura

© Central de arquitectura

197   The use of glass is the most effective way of integrating a terrace with the rest of the home. Large windows should be made of reflective glass or glass that has been treated with a metallic coating. This type of material reduces the heat from the sun, protects the interior from UV light and creates an attractive mirror effect.

The interior spaces are free of obstructions that could obscure the dialog between the interior and the exterior. They spill onto the pool and shaded outdoors dining area effortlessly.

© Daniel Levin

© Tim Griffith

This property combines large glazed areas with natural mahogany wood cladding on the façade. This same type of wood is used to cover the entire area around the swimming pool.

© Tim Griffith

© John Linden

© John Linden

© John Linden

198 Look for consistency in your interior and exterior styles. Your outdoor space is another room in your home and you need to care for it and understand it as such in order for it to be fully integrated.

© Giorgio Possenti

199

Don't just stick to plants when it comes to decorating a terrace. Spectacular walls, such as the one in the photo, and elements such as ceramics, sculptures and water features also work well in outdoor spaces.

© Turett Collaborative Architects

© Fabrizio Miccò

200 As the plot is completely filled, the roof has become central in order to provide communal outdoors space. The result is a lush garden with wide open and secluded zones.

© Ben Wrigley

The separate functions of this stylish ground-level terrace are clearly defined. The lap pool is sectioned off with a glass partition, and the eating area is protected with a canopy.

© Ben Wrigley

© João Morgado – Architecture Photography

201 Microcement flooring is a good choice for giving your terrace a modern feel. Although they are more commonly used inside than out, their impervious nature is leading them to be used increasingly in outdoor areas around swimming pools. They are easy to lay and clean, and maintenance is very cheap. There is also a wide selection of colors to choose from.

Not just a house in the air. The architects say it walks on water. And it does: on the Mediterranean, although far away. The pool brings the water to the house.

© Diego Opazo

© Patrick Bingham-Hall

The sense of scale in the courtyard is carefully
regulated: the archipelago of parterres and trees
that occupy the space are the center of attention.

202

The building is terraced allowing each storey to have visual and physical connection with a landscaped area. This creates a layer effect that reduces the scale of the building.

© Patrick Bingham-Hall